GOO

© Ronald Brown

World rights reserved worldwide by the publishers

Arthur James Limited
One Cranbourne Road
London N10 2BT
Great Britain

First published 1992

British Library Cataloguing-in-Publication Data

Brown, Ronald
Good Lord: A Light-hearted Sketch of a Ministry
I. Title
827.91408

ISBN 0-85305-326-X

Illustrations by Graeme Skinner

Cover Design by
The Creative House, Saffron Walden, Essex

Typeset by Stumptype, London N20

Printed and bound by
The Guernsey Press, Guernsey, Channel Islands

GOOD LORD

A Light-hearted Sketch of a Ministry

by

RONALD BROWN

Former Bishop of Birkenhead
Author of Bishop's Brew

To Barry & Jennifer
With affectionate good
wishes.
+ Ronald Birkenhead

Arthur James
BOOK PUBLISHERS

Dedicated To Those Who Shared These Days:

Mark Brown

Janet Artingstall

and, of course,

Joyce
(RIP)

CONTENTS

CHAPTER ONE

"A Curate — there is something which excites
compassion in the very name of a Curate!"
(Sydney Smith 1771-1845)

Perspiration was running down my face like water from a
shower as I jumped up and down and clapped my hands over
my head in my first PT Class in years. My glasses were
steamed up and I was breathing hard. There was a strong
temptation to stop for a minute and take off the brand-new
clerical collar that felt as if it were choking me, but I resisted
it. I had already removed my coat, but for reasons of decorum
felt the collar should stay. Even after just one day in the parish
I had got the strong impression that Curates were expected
to behave with restraint and dignity.

The dog-collar was somehow a symbol of this and certainly
seemed to be treated with special veneration by the lay folk.
The day before, after my Ordination, an old lady had said
how disappointed she was that the Bishop had not actually
put the collar round my neck during the Service. "Are you
sure you've been properly done?" she asked in all seriousness.

I reassured her about the validity of the rite in spite of the
omission, but she didn't look too sure about it as she fired
a further question. "Tell me," she asked, "are you ever
allowed to take it off?". I treated her to a limerick that had
gone the rounds in my Theological College:

There once was a Curate who said
"May I take off my collar in bed?"
The Bishop said, "No! Wherever you go,
You'll wear it until you are dead."

She joined in the laughter before wagging a finger under

my nose as she issued an admonition: "There you are then, make sure you do what the Bishop said."

The old lady came from my home parish, twenty miles from Chorley where I had come to serve my title — that's how a clergyman's first job is described — but I knew the people here would be just as traditional. Not that they were at all stuffy, for they were well endowed with the gifts of welcome and friendship.

And now here I was making my first contact with the Church Lads' Brigade as it met in the hall of the parochial school just across the road from where I lived. After introducing me to the boys, (there were about thirty of them present), George, the officer-in-charge, had started the evening's activities with some physical training exercises. I decided it might get me off to a good start if I volunteered to join in, and after a couple of minutes was bitterly regretting the decision.

Huffing and puffing like a man of fifty-five rather than twenty-five, I was secretly resolving to give up the Woodbines, when to my relief there came an interruption that put an end to our physical jerks for a while. A loud crashing noise in an adjacent classroom was so violent that we all automatically froze on the spot. George raised his hand and motioned the class to the side of the hall where there were chairs: "Break off for a few minutes, lads," he said, "sit over there and try to be reasonably quiet." With a flick of the head he signalled me to follow as he went to investigate.

We saw at once the cause of the noise. There was a large jagged hole in one of the gothic-type windows. Since the damage had been done from the inside there was not much broken glass and debris on the floor, but the bit that was there lay around the feet of a boy who was grinning broadly and looking as proud as punch at what he had done. About fourteen years of age, he had his hair plastered down with grease, and although in a good suit, he looked decidedly scruffy and half-washed.

"Sorry," he said, though his attitude suggested he didn't know the meaning of the word, "sorry, but my foot slipped while I was practising dribbling."

George was plainly furious. "You are a stupid boy," he shouted. "You know you're not supposed to play football inside the school: now we'll have yet another serious complaint from the headmaster." He turned and spoke to me. "This is Kevin Butler, Mr. Brown: he should have been in the PT Class in the hall with the rest of them, but he's not only stupid, he's a lazy blighter as well."

The grin quickly disappeared from Kevin's face and was replaced by a scowl. When he spoke it was out of the corner of his mouth for extra derision. "Wrap up! Who do you think you're calling stupid? Anybody can make a mistake. I tell you I was only practising a bit of soccer and my foot slipped. But if that's your attitude you can get stuffed, and that goes for the Church Lads' Brigade too."

He felt in his pocket and produced a crumpled packet of cigarettes. A rather battered-looking fag was extracted and popped into his mouth. As he turned to walk away, he felt in his pocket for a match.

What followed took me completely by surprise. George's hand flicked out like the tongue of a rattlesnake, not only knocking the cigarette flying, but also landing with some force on Kevin's face. It was to be a night of surprises, for the next move was even more unexpected.

Kevin swung round, tears in his eyes, half crying, half smarting with anger: he pointed an accusing finger at me. "You shouldn't have done that," he screamed, "Vicars aren't allowed to hit people, it's against the law: you could be un... un... un-something for that." Having failed to find the word 'unfrocked' he resorted to a more natural phraseology. "Kicked out, kicked out, that's what you should be."

I tried to get a word in edgeways to protest my innocence but it was no use, he wasn't listening. Too busy, in fact, issuing further threats. "You just wait, Holy Joe, till mi dad gets you;

5

he'll break your flippin' neck and have your guts for garters.''
With more bloodcurdling promises he made his exit, taking
with him a red weal on the side of his face that quite alarmed
me.

His route to the main door took him through the hall where
the rest of the boys watched and listened in awe. I could hear
him shouting to them as he sped by. ''The new Curate's mad,
should be locked up, look what he's done to my face.''

I walked back with George to where they were. In a whisper
I asked him whether this kind of thing happened often. ''Do
you actually clout them on a regular basis?'' I enquired.

George laughed. ''Good Lord, no,'' he said with a grin.
'In fact I've never done it before but that kid made me so
mad. I didn't intend to hit his face at all, just meant to clip
his ear; but, if you'll pardon the expression, my hand slipped
a bit! But don't worry about it, he'll get over it and I'll bet
you he's back here next week you just see.''

I was genuinely relieved to hear that physical violence was
not part of the stock-in-trade. I had had a horror of pain being
inflicted in the name of religion ever since my school-days,
when an RE teacher had seemed to enjoy hitting people over
the head with a Bible to emphasise his points. For an
important bit of instruction you could get a knock for each
word. ''Thou-shalt-love-thy-neighbour-as-thyself'' could leave
you with a headache for the rest of the day. I was glad to know
that there was nothing like that in this organisation. I wanted
to be a friend to the boys, not a stern authoritarian figure.

I walked over to a group of them by the side of the hall.
As one man, they took a pace backwards, and two or three
of them at the front raised their arms in a gesture of self-
defence. They were obviously convinced that Kevin had
correctly identified his assailant. I turned on a big smile to
try to reassure them. ''Come on lads,'' I said, ''I just want
to get to know you and be friends.'' I moved towards them
again. Again they retreated a yard. I was at a loss to know
how to handle the situation and I stood there awkwardly,

relieved at last to hear George calling them back on parade.

"C-o-m-p-a-n-y, Fall In!" he bawled in his best sergeant-major voice. I noticed that as my group joined the others in the middle, they kept an arm's length distance from me as they filed past, obviously making sure that I didn't lash out at them as they thought I had at Kevin. Me, that literally wouldn't hurt a fly! I was mortified.

I sat on a chair and watched them line up in columns of three. I certainly didn't intend to march up and down the hall with them. In fact, I wondered why on earth they wanted to do that either, but before long I was to learn that the programme of uniform, drill, games, badges, bands and parades was exactly suited to the healthy physique and average intelligence of the boys who enrolled. I discovered too, that with the right kind of leadership, other subjects and activities could be introduced to enrich the fellowship and the usefulness of the meetings. George had been a soldier in General Montgomery's desert army; he was smart, athletic and resourceful. He was now on the verge of starting the marching. "Company, by the left ..." He was interrupted before he could complete the command.

"Please Sir," said a boy in the front rank holding up his hand, "there's somebody at the door."

"Go and see who it is."

In half a minute he was back. "It's a woman, Sir, wants the Curate."

As I left the room to find out what it was all about, the marchers finally got under way. Behind me I could hear, "Left, Right, Left, Right," and the sound of marching feet, as I got to the door and peered into the fading light. I addressed the shadowy figure of a woman on the doorstep. "Yes? I believe you want me."

"Well, as a matter of fact, I don't," came the unexpected reply, "but beggars can't be choosers, and I'm told you are the only clergyman available."

I looked closer and saw a tall thin woman in her mid-fifties, wearing a navy-blue gaberdine coat edged in red. A nurse's pill-box hat sat on top of her grey hair which was gathered together severely in a bun at the back. She spoke very haughtily as she explained why she had come, nose in the air, with a few sniffs to emphasise her superiority.

"I am the Assistant Matron of The Park Avenue Nursing Home, and I urgently need a clergyman."

"Well, believe it or not, you've found one: a brand new one I admit, but a real one nevertheless," I said rather tetchily. "What can I do for you?"

In a condescending fashion she explained that an old lady in the Home had died a few hours before. The undertaker had been and "attended to her", so now it was appropriate that a clergyman should come and "do the usual things".

"I suppose you do know what to do?" she asked with the biggest sniff so far. And then as though speaking to herself she continued, "I only wish I could have got hold of a proper clergyman, but I've been to the Rectory and Canon Wyatt is away. I've tried to get Mr. Povey the retired priest, but he's in bed with flu. They told me at the Rectory to get you." She looked at me with obvious disdain.

I suddenly became aware that I must have looked a bit of a mess. I had been wiping the sweat off my face with my hands and I could see they were filthy from the dust of the school. I stood there in my shirtsleeves with the new black stock hanging out of my pullover. My hair was all over the place. I ran my hands through it to straighten it and then started to tuck in the stock.

"I'll come with you at once," I said as I turned to pick up my coat from a peg in the entrance. I put it on as I walked quickly to catch her up, rubbing my face and hands on a handkerchief in an attempt to smarten myself up a bit. As I pushed it back into a pocket it was good to feel there was a Prayer Book there too. That was one piece of advice from my College Principal that had quickly paid dividends. I remembered he had also advised us in the same lecture never to be alone with a woman if we could avoid it. "If one comes into your vestry," he had said, "make sure you keep the door open, otherwise scandal may ensue." I was glad of his advice to carry a copy of the Prayer Book around, but I didn't think his caution regarding amorous women applied to this harridan whom I was chasing after in the street.

"I thought you might have gone home first to er, er, wash, or something," she said when I caught up with her. I made no reply. "You may call me Miss Murphy," she went on, as though bestowing a royal privilege. "The Matron is away for a few days and I am in sole charge: one just has to accept these responsibilities." I was thinking, "Gosh, if she's only the Assistant Matron, what must the boss-woman be like!"

We hadn't far to go, maybe half a mile from the school. She used every yard of it to rub home her disquiet at getting a novice for an important job. "Three Rectors I have known, all good and able men," she explained: "cannot remember how many Curates, and most of them are best forgotten anyway, two a penny, if you ask me. Makes you wonder what the Church is coming to."

Her tirade was doing nothing for my morale. As a matter of fact I felt in urgent need of the opposite kind of treatment for I was distinctly uneasy at what lay ahead. For one thing, I had never seen a dead body before, and not to put too fine a point on it, was more than a bit apprehensive at the prospect of being in the presence of a corpse. And then there was another even weightier thing troubling me. I hadn't the foggiest idea what to do when I got there.

I could have produced six sound reasons for believing in the after-life; I could have described the structure and history of the Burial Service; but what to do when confronted with a dead body was completely unknown territory. I could at a pinch have coped with a bed-side visit to someone actually dying, but I told myself it was jolly hard luck to be called out for the very first time to deal with something completely outside my experience. And to have a she-dragon hovering over my shoulder at the same time didn't help. At that moment, I wondered whether the Church of England had got its training methods right. Its system is to deal with the academic side of things in College, and then with just a smattering of what is called 'pastoralia', its new clergy are sent out to learn the trade in a parish under an experienced priest. It obviously believes that 'smiting makes the smith', but alas, here I was being asked to shoe a horse before I even knew what an anvil looked like!

We finally arrived at what had been at one time a large semi-detached residence. In the fading light I saw the blue-and-gold notice-board that indicated its present use. Miss Murphy used her key and I followed her into the entrance hall. "How long will you need?" she asked in a quieter voice than I had heard so far.

I was tempted to say, "I haven't the foggiest," but instead heard myself replying in measured tones, "I normally need about a quarter of an hour." It sounded reasonably professional and confident — the very qualities that were so sadly lacking.

"Come this way," she commanded, and I started to climb the wide stairs behind her.

If she had set out to create an eerie atmosphere she couldn't have done it better. The only illumination came from two large candles standing in oak candlesticks, presumably provided by the funeral director, and placed one at the head, the other at the foot, of the coffin. This stood on trestles covered with a purple pall in the middle of the room. Miss Murphy moved aside to let me go in first.

"Make sure you do it properly," she hissed as I passed her: "remember, a lot depends on it." She made it sound as though heaven or hell would be determined by my ministrations. It went through my mind that some people must have a very odd idea of what God is like if they can conceive for an instant that the eternal destiny of a person can be resolved by some ritualistic act, no matter how ancient or elaborate. There was no place for magic in my ecclesiastical repertoire. That would be too much at variance with the picture of God that came from Jesus Christ. I had learned enough about Anglican theology to appreciate that that was always the touchstone. I remembered that one of my college tutors had put this in very strong terms. "You must never say that Jesus is like God," he had advised, "always say that God is like Jesus."

With some apprehension I started to take in the scene. Then, out of the corner of my eye, I saw the door begin to close with Miss Murphy on the outside. With just her face visible she spoke again: "I'll lock you in, then you won't be disturbed; some of our elderly patients wander about sometimes." I heard the key turn in the lock.

I was relieved she wasn't going to stand over me. I made the sign of the Cross over myself, partly in gratitude for that, partly to allay my unease. That acted prayer brought its usual reassurance. I started to advance rather gingerly towards the coffin in the flickering light. Unfortunately the lady had failed to warn me that she had placed a stool alongside, on which presumably I was expected to kneel. It caught me just below the knees, and I fell forwards with hands outstretched towards the coffin. I grabbed at a small table in front of me for support, knocking over a vase of flowers in the process. With one hand on the table and the other on the coffin I righted myself, and for the first time looked at the body. Only the face was visible; it was very, very old, peaceful and serene. The rest of the body was covered in white satin with lace at the edges.

My eyes were coping better with the dim light by this time, and I could see that the water from the vase had caused some splashing on the satin shroud just below the face. I picked up the vase and its contents, and with my already soiled and damp handkerchief mopped up as much of the mess as I could from the table and the carpet. I refilled the vase with water from a wash-basin I had spotted in the corner, and did my best with the subsequent flower arranging. A dab or two with my coat sleeve on the table-top and the side of the coffin

11

completed my efforts to eliminate all traces of my clumsiness. I shuddered to think what Miss Murphy would make of it all.

Then it was down to business. I fished out the Prayer Book, stood by the top candle, and recited aloud Psalm 23. It's not the best-known Psalm for nothing. Its words have a remarkable power to calm and reassure the faint-hearted in all kinds of difficult situations.

> "The Lord is my shepherd: therefore can I lack nothing."

Talk about positive thinking linked to spiritual truth! As I said the familiar words, I knew there was no better prayer for the old lady in the whole world than this.

> "Yea though I walk through the valley of the shadow of death, I will fear no evil; for thou art with me."

Although it comes from the Old Testament, it was good to remember that Jesus had lifted it to a new significance by referring to Himself as the 'Good Shepherd'. The connection is underlined by the fact that the word used for 'Good' did not mean morally good, but rather 'good to have', or attractive. One famous scholar (William Temple) even translates Jesus' words, "I am the shepherd, the beautiful one".

It occurred to me that if I didn't say anything else in that place of death it wouldn't matter. To ask for the presence and forgiveness of Jesus for someone as they cross the river from this world to the next is surely the prayer *par excellence*; and to do it with such an affirmation of trust seemed to me to be in keeping with Jesus' own instruction on how to make prayer really work. "I tell you then," Jesus had said, "whatever you ask for in prayer, believe that you have received it, and it will be yours."

I didn't leave it at that though, for I found it easier than I had expected to cobble together a little service with various strands in it. There was the Lord's Prayer, of course, for that fits any situation, and special intentions can enrich every clause. I prayed for God's comfort and consolation for bereaved folk; I thanked God for the life of the old lady; and then I used the old commendation from my Prayer Book:

Go forth upon thy journey from this world, O
Christian soul,
In the name of God the Father Almighty who
created thee.
In the name of Jesus Christ who suffered for thee.
In the name of the Holy Spirit who strengtheneth
thee.
In communion with the blessed Saints, and aided by
Angels and Archangels, and all the armies of the
heavenly host.
May thy portion this day be in peace, and thy
dwelling in the heavenly Jerusalem.   Amen.

The sign of the Cross was made over the body as I pronounced the final Blessing. Then I raised the other arm to the candle so that I could see my watch more clearly. A quick calculation told me it would be another five or six minutes before I could expect to be released. I walked over to an arm-chair by the door and was glad to be able to flop into it. It had been quite an evening. I hadn't realised how tired I was.

I tried to relax but found it difficult, wondering why, like so many, I was uneasy in the presence of a dead body. Even the word 'death' is avoided whenever possible by some. They talk about grandad being 'no longer with us'; or grandma 'having passed away'; words like the 'departed' or the 'deceased' are used in the same process of circumlocution. Sitting there I smiled as I remembered some children who lived near me at one time, telling me that Rusty (their large ferocious mongrel that tried to bite not only the postman every day, but everybody else within reach) had met its demise. Their announcement was couched in euphemistic terms as they said, "Our Rusty has gone to live with Jesus." I have never really wrestled with the theological implications of their claim, but I understand some were able to accept the proposition readily enough, and the postman was not the only one to greet the news with a loud "Amen"!

My musings continued along the same lines. Maybe there was a perfectly rational explanation for our distaste and fear. Could it be, I wondered, an inherited mental attitude, deeply engrained in the human psyche, having its origin in those times when dead bodies were thought to be dangerous, full of the plague, or of anthrax, or of some other infectious desease? Several times in the Old Testament it is made clear that "He that toucheth the dead body of any man shall be unclean seven days" (Numbers 19, verse 11). In Haggai 2, verse 13, the question is asked, "If one that is unclean by a dead body touch any of these (foods), shall it be unclean? And the priests answered and said, It shall be unclean."

However, most Biblical scholars believe this type of uncleanness had nothing to do with the modern idea of hygiene and health but was concerned with religious ritual and taboos. I decided all this had probably very little to do with our strange aversion.

I cast around for a more likely explanation. I hit on another possibility. Few of us like being reminded of our mortality, and a dead body certainly does that. But surely, I mused, there is no excuse for such a reaction among Christians. It is not as though belief in the after-life is an optional extra, just tacked on at the end of the Creed. It is there at the very beginning when we acknowledge God as our heavenly Father. What sort of a father is it that snuffs out the life of his child as though it does not matter?

The shortest verse in the New Testament contains two words only, "Jesus wept". They were said at the graveside of Lazarus, and the only reason for the tears was the terrible effect his death had had on family and friends. All so unnecessary! Maybe Jesus was also looking into the future and seeing those countless other families and friends that would be similarly devastated by the death of a loved one. He did all that was humanly (and divinely) possible to save us from this and convince us of life beyond the grave. After all, you cannot do more than die publicly on a Cross and then come back and show yourself to people, can you? And He gave His solemn promise: "Because I live, ye shall live also". No wonder the New Testament writers are vibrant with the certainty of it all.

My thoughts were disturbed by the rustling of the long velvet curtains in the bay-window. Until then I had not realised the window was open. Maybe the open window was just a coincidence, but it came to mind that some folk in my native Lancashire always left a window open in such a room, whatever the time of year. They argued there must be free passage for the newly released spirit. They would keep the main door of the house ajar too for the same reason. Only ajar, not open, for that would be to risk other spirits coming in to take up residence. It struck me that this might be an area of experience also responsible to some extent for generating and shaping the fear and abhorrence of dead bodies. Ghosts and hauntings, demons and devils, and all the rest of the genre, strike terror into many hearts.

I knew that any minute now Miss Murphy would be back. I stood up in readiness. It would not do to let her find me lolling in a chair.

I made myself take a last look at the coffin and its contents. I was not exactly frightened, just a bit uneasy. I felt sure an old aunt of mine would have been relieved to see the eyes so firmly closed. She always recounted the local superstition that if they were difficult to close it was because the dead person was looking for someone to follow them quickly into the grave. There was a whole collection of these weird tales, passed on with half a smile, half a shiver. For instance, all the mirrors in a place of death had to be covered, otherwise those visiting spirits coming to provide an escort might become visible. All the curtains in a house had to be drawn too, not merely as a sign of sadness, but because at such a time there was an increase in psychic activity, and malicious spooks might look in and be tempted to make their abode there. It was even said that the practice of carrying the body out "feet first" was to stop the newly-released spirit from seeing clearly so that it could not find its way back to haunt the place.

What a load of codswallop it all was, I thought, and what a lovely thing to be able to help people jettison such burdens in the name of Christ. St Paul must have been doing this for some early Christians who lived in Rome when he wrote in a letter to them, "I am convinced that there is nothing in death or life, in the realm of spirits or superhuman powers, in the world as it is or the world as it shall be, in the forces of the universe, in heights or depths — nothing in all creation that can separate us from the love of God in Christ Jesus our Lord."

I still jumped a bit when the key turned in the lock with a loud click. The door opened and Miss Murphy moved in. "Finished?" she asked, looking first at me and then at the coffin. She obviously had eyes like a hawk, "Oh, it's all wet," she exclaimed, and my heart sank. I had hoped she would not notice. "All wet," she continued, "now that's a surprise." There was a pause while she put two and two together and made twenty-two! Then she added, "You've been using holy water, haven't you? That's a turn-up for the book, I didn't think you'd know how to do it." She positively beamed with pleasure.

I was too astonished to say a word. I stood there open-mouthed.

By now the woman was gushing. "So pleased you spotted the wash-basin, but I notice you have left the tap dripping slightly." She crossed the room and turned the tap an extra millimetre. "The priest from my church, St Peter's, always uses holy water," she informed me, "I'll tell him he has a kindred spirit in the town now. I really am pleased with you. You know these things do make a difference, don't they?"

Alas, out of sheer cowardice I remained speechless. The voice of conscience told me this was tantamount to lying. I cleared my throat ready to confess. It was not going to be easy. "Well, actually ..." I began, "it is not quite ..."

Miss Murphy butted in with more compliments. "Well done, well done. I am so sorry I misjudged you, Mr. Brown, maybe I was even a little brusque when we first met." She gave a twittering laugh.

I wanted to say, "A little brusque? Rubbish! You were damned rude." I bit my tongue and stayed silent. I knew clergymen were not supposed to say 'damn' anyhow. As we came downstairs together I made a deal with my conscience. The two silences cancelled each other out, so to speak, for if cowardice had brought me undeserved credit, I had on the plus side avoided being unnecessarily rude to the Assistant Matron. I felt it was a reasonable deal.

The friendliness was getting almost embarrassing as we made our way downstairs. "I've got a feeling you'll be a very good priest in time, with the right training and with greater maturity, but you must always do things the right way, no short-cuts, no sloppiness. Now, you must let me get you a nice cup of tea."

"No thanks," I said quickly. By this time we were in the hall and I was holding the handle of the front door. Alas, it would have been more Christian to depart in silence, but the old Adam within me could not refrain from a parting shot.

I opened the door ready to go. "Thank you for offering me tea, Miss Murphy. That was the right thing to do. Well done. However, since the Rector is away, I am in sole charge of the parish and there are many things that need my attention; one just has to accept these responsibilities. Good night."

The icy glare and muted reply indicated that the sarcasm had not gone unnoticed. I stepped out into the night air with more relief than I can express. I was in a self-congratulatory mood as I walked home; "Game, Set, and Match," I said aloud. It was the kind of euphoria I was to experience many times in the years ahead, the kind that comes from the release of tension when something difficult or unpleasant has been accomplished. I walked with a light step as I rehearsed the story I would tell Joyce, my wife of a year, over supper. I knew she would appreciate every detail.

I stepped from the street into the yard at the rear of the house and made for the steps that led to the back door, normally kept unlocked. The yard gate swung shut behind me with a dull thud. I had got one foot on the bottom step when a heavy hand landed on my shoulder. Extremely startled, I turned to see a burly figure in what looked like a boiler-suit. By the street light from over the wall I could see he was rough and unkempt, and when he pushed his face close to mine I could smell beer on his breath. My first thought was that this was a tramp after money. I was soon disabused of such an innocent explanation.

. "Have you been thumping our Kevin ?" the man growled. I went weak at the knees and felt sick. My voice sounded at least an octave higher than usual as I replied.

"Er ... well ... I was involved in a bit of trouble earlier tonight, but you can take it from me your Kevin asked for it." I swallowed hard, and pulled my shoulder away. I was relieved when he allowed his hand to fall clear. I got both feet on the bottom step and turned to face him, now almost as tall as he was. He raised a fist, but not to strike, just for emphasis. He pushed it perilously close to my chin, and held it there while he made his statement.

The words were music to my ears. "You say he asked for it; I guessed as much. He's a cheeky little devil. His mother's to blame, turned him into a spoilt brat, she has. And what I want to say to you Mr. Brown, is this: belt him whenever you think he needs it. I'd be glad if somebody would knock some sense and manners into him. I'm not allowed to

raise a finger to him, but by heaven, he needs it."

My heart was still pounding a bit, but the sense of relief was enormous. I had thought I was in for either a black eye or, at best, the threat of a law-suit. I took a deep breath and summoned up my last bit of courage for the night. My voice still did not sound right and my throat was dry.

"That's all very well Mr. Butler, but what about the damage? Who's going to foot the bill?" I felt embarrassed at pressing the matter but knew I had to do it. I did not fancy the alternative of forking out myself.

He took a step back while he pondered the matter. "To tell you the truth I'm more or less stony at the moment," he said at last, "but listen, I have putty and glass, and I'll fix it myself tomorrow after work. I'll make a good job of it, I'll not let you down. Tell the caretaker I'll be round about half-past five. Now will that do you?"

I could not do other than accept the offer. I said goodnight and was about to climb the steps when the heavy hand descended again. I hoped he was more gentle when handling the glass. The beer fumes reappeared in my nostrils.

"Remember, Mr. Brown, lay into him when he gets out of hand. I'll back you a hundred per cent. Don't want him in trouble with the police like his brother."

I just nodded and was anxious not to prolong the conversation. I was on the second step when he turned for a final word. "I'll tell you what, Mr. Brown, you've made a big hit with the lads." (I did not think the pun was intended.) "Half a dozen of them always come round to our house at the end of the CLB Meeting, and by gum, they think you're great. You know, they don't like namby-pambies. They think you'll be as good as the last Curate — he was a tough guy. By the way, is it true you were the boxing champion of your College?"

For a moment I was tempted; but then decided I had been involved in enough lies for one night. "No, it is not true," I replied, "but I was president of the literary and debating society." Completely inconsequential but, at least, true!

He obviously did not know what to make of that and shuffled off through the gate. Wearily I staggered into the house. Joyce was doing the ironing in the kitchen. She produced a cup of tea and I sat for a while watching her while I drank it.

She thoroughly enjoyed my account of the evening's happenings. The iron had to be put down once or twice so that she could laugh heartily and safely. She did not interrupt once. She was a good listener. At the end of my narrative she said she thought I deserved a tasty supper. In a short space we were sitting round the kitchen table with Welsh rarebit in front of us.

As we dined I remarked that if the last few hours were anything to go by it looked as though we were in for a strange life. "What a beginning!" I exclaimed.

It was a short time later as we stood by the sink doing the washing-up that the same words came back into my head.

"You know, Joyce," I said, "if I had to find a text to describe my experiences today I think I would opt for the first four words of the Bible: 'In the beginning God'."

She made no comment, so I went on to expound the theme. "I feel God has been in my beginning, rescuing me out of one or two rather tricky situations. Yes, I'll settle for that. 'In the beginning God'."

I got a very quizzical look as she folded the tea-towel over the edge of the draining-board. "Surely you're not serious?" she asked. "I call what's happened to you today beginners' luck, and the thing to remember about that is it doesn't last. For goodness sake, don't turn into a 'God-botherer'; He's more important things to do than go round righting your mistakes." She laughed as she spoke to lighten the message, but I knew it was an instance of many a true word being spoken in jest.

Before we went to bed she returned to the subject. "You were wrong about the Bible," she said, "it doesn't begin with a sentence of four words." She held up the fingers of both hands for emphasis: "There are ten words in the first sentence. I think half the trouble in religion is caused by people putting fullstops in the Bible where they don't exist. Things have to be kept in context." She recited the ten words in question: 'In the beginning God created the heaven and the earth'. "To me," she went on, "that means that God has made everything in heaven and earth, and we have to accept the whole of life, in all its fulness, the things we like and the things we don't. I reckon we'll have our share of both, don't you?"

"I thought I was the one paid to preach sermons in this parish," I replied facetiously.

"I'm going upstairs now," she said, "don't forget to put the lights out when you come to bed."

Before doing so, I sat in a chair by the fireside for five minutes. I agreed mainly with what she had said; sometimes I enjoyed goading her into action. I knew she disliked what she called the 'holy, holy' approach.

Even so, it was a strange job I had got myself. Not a job like any other, I reflected. I went back to the way Christ had called the first Apostles. He had not offered them a job as such; He had not said, "This is what you have to do, and these are the results you will get, and these are the conditions of service". It was not like that at all. He had simply called them to be with Him, to share in His mission and ministry. Other folk could and should feel called to their work in life: doctors, teachers, plumbers, the lot. Yet, it seemed to me in my meditation that my job was in the last resort not a call to a profession but to Him, to share in His work as a shepherd of souls.

I recalled the Ordination Service of the previous day. One of the Bishop's questions was still fresh in my mind. "Do you think you are truly called, according to the will of our Lord Jesus Christ to the Ministry of the Church?"

I loved the modest reply the Prayer Book had put into my

22

mouth: "I think so" I had said.

I put the lights out and climbed the stairs in the dark. Somehow it seemed a bit symbolic.

CHAPTER TWO

"Christ's lore, and His Apostles twelve, He taught,
but first He practised it Himself."
(The Poor Parson: Geoffrey Chaucer 1340-1400)

It is always embarrassing to see a man weep in public. More
so when that person is normally very composed, dignified
and even authoritarian. And when such an occurrence does
not just happen once, but repeatedly and regularly over a
period of nearly twelve months, then the embarrassment starts
to give way to irritation and annoyance. The whole thing is
intensified in importance when the person in question is a
priest, who sometimes behaves in this way in front of two
or three hundred people as he stands in the pulpit or before
the Altar.

Canon Wyatt had lost his wife a few months before I joined
him as Curate, and although he put on a brave face when
dealing with people on a one-to-one basis, his emotions got
the better of him time and again as he prayed for 'the faithful
departed' in the Communion Service, or found himself in a
sermon dealing with such subjects as family life, human love,
life after death, or any one of a dozen things that triggered
off thoughts of his dead wife. Certainly he could not get
through either the funeral service or the wedding service
without an emotional interruption.

On any of these occasions he would stand there unable to
go on, shoulders shaking with emotion, tears running down
his cheeks, pretending to blow his nose with a handkerchief
held in front of his face. After one or two false starts, his
normally well-modulated voice would crack a few times before
finally getting going again, taking up from where he had left
off.

Everybody was touched by his sadness and loneliness. They would remind one another, "He hasn't got a single living relative in the whole world." They also knew he lived in a great barn of a house, and that he had few, if any, close friends. He was also hard-working and good at his job. It would be true to say he was held in great respect rather than great affection, though those who got to know him best liked him very much, and everybody valued his professional and efficient ministry.

This did not stop people from saying before long that they wished he would pull himself together, and a few were beginning to whisper that maybe it was time he retired. "He needs a rest," they said, "time to get over his wife's death; and the parish does need an active, younger man."

Those who had his real welfare at heart knew that was the last thing he needed, but in most parishes there are inevitably a few people who look forward to a change of priest, and this particular group did have, at that time, a special opportunity to press their claim.

My difficulty was knowing what to do about the situation. Canon Wyatt was my boss rather than my friend, and there was a gap of more than forty years in our ages. A stickler for professional etiquette, he would have resented advice or admonition from a very junior colleague. At that stage, there was no special warmth in our relationship either, as was demonstrated once after a children's service. A little girl on her way out asked the Rector, "Are you Mr. Brown's daddy?" He denied it with a degree of revulsion that would have been not inappropriate in a denial of membership of the IRA!

Perhaps things would have been easier had I played cricket, for although in his late sixties when I joined him, he was still captain of the Diocesan eleven, and I am sure I would not have got the job as his assistant had there been a slow-left-arm bowler among the candidates! He was only about five foot six, but he carried himself well and walked tall. Although he used a walking-stick regularly, it was clear from the

25

way he brandished it that its purpose was decorative rather than utilitarian. He was broad shouldered, had a handsome face, and his greying hair was parted in the middle and brushed straight back. He generally looked serious, even stern.

Canon Wyatt had been ordained more than forty years before in Manchester Cathedral, at the very same service as my old Grammar School Headmaster, and he tended to deal with me in much the same way. I addressed him as "Sir", and he called me "Brown". He boasted that he did not suffer fools gladly, and most folk treated him with great respect, even awe. This went for his fellow clergy too, for he was Rural Dean as well as Rector, and woe betide any priest who dared to step out of line at a Deanery Conference or Chapter Meeting. "Sit down, sit down, Mr Whittaker," he would bellow, "we've had enough of that." Or, "No, no, you may not speak Mr Samuels. We know what you're going to say anyway, and I'm not going to allow you to waste our time." He could glare the rest of the brethren into silence.

Yet here was this strong, lonely man needing help, and I was at a loss to know how it could be provided. Joyce and I talked about it often. Her advice was invariably the same. "Give him time, more time, it really does heal in the end; and if anybody complains to you about his public weeping, tell them to mind their own business." She was nothing if not direct! This fitted my own instincts and inclinations. Then came a dramatic incident that I have remembered vividly ever since.

The Canon and I were in the Vestry taking our robes off after a mid-week Communion Service. There had been an emotional interruption half way through, but lasting only a very short time. I was thinking about something entirely different when Bill, the Verger, came bursting in at his usual breakneck speed carrying the chalice and paten which he had just removed from the altar.

Bill was a great character valued by everybody. Well past seventy, he still had boundless energy, always half running, half walking, as he moved around his beloved church. With a chuckle, he would say in his broad Lancashire accent that he was built as a whippet, a not altogether inappropriate description for this small, thin, wiry man who had been Verger for donkey's years. Under a wisp of straggly grey hair, he wore round, horn-rimmed spectacles perched on the edge of a rather large bulbous nose. His false teeth, like their owner, were ever on the move, and whenever he laughed, which was often, his top set dropped like a trap-door, preventing any further sound until it was hitched up again with an index finger. Admittedly no oil painting, but a lovely man who served church and people well.

Now he walked over to the sink in the corner, turned on the tap, and began to wash the vessels. With the background noise of running water he suddenly started his speech.

"Aye Rector, I've something to say to thee." He put the chalice down on the dripboard, turned off the tap and walked over so that he was directly in front of Wyatt. I got the impression that he had been plucking up courage for this moment — his face was slightly flushed.

"I'm getting sick and tired of all this yelling thou does for thi missus."

I thought, "Good grief! What a way to begin. If only the floor would open and swallow me up". I was actually looking in the opposite direction of the floor, at the ceiling in fact, and as an alternative would have been willing to levitate through that. But since there was no escape, I did not move a muscle as I waited for Bill's homily to continue.

I had not long to wait. He took a deep breath and plunged in again. "When my missus died ten year sin', thou told me she'd gone to heaven." The dialect thickened as he got more excited. "Thou said I had to pull misel' together, show I'ad a bit o' faith i' God. Well now, I'm tellin' thee t'same. Pu' thysel' together, have a sup o' thi own medicine. A fella in thy position hasn't only to tell 'em about Christianity, but show 'em. And I don't mean next week, I mean now."

That was it. Not another word. There was complete silence for nearly a minute, and the three of us stood absolutely still. I stole a glance at the Rector. I could see he was angry. The notorious glower was in position, the atmosphere electric. I could see he was on the point of shouting, "How dare you!" However, instead he swallowed hard, turned round to the desk behind him, picked up a pen, and started to sign the Service Register. Still with his back to both of us, his muffled voice eventually said just three words "Thank you, Bill."

This broke the spell and Bill walked over to the corner once more where he got on with his job of washing the chalice. I grabbed my coat and beat a hasty retreat.

I disliked being embarrassed like that but it turned out to have been worthwhile for the treatment worked the oracle. Never again did the Rector weep in public. In fact, I was able to look back on that scene in the Vestry as a real turning point. Within a few weeks he had taken up golf with some of his clerical colleagues; he had become interested in bee-keeping again; and for the first time since I had known him, there was a lightness about his step, a greater willingness to smile, and a more relaxed attitude to others, not least to me.

Although he never referred directly to the event, I thought once or twice he had it in mind when he gave me advice about communicating the Gospel in my work as a priest. "The most important things you say, Brown, are not said in a pulpit, but to individuals, personally, and often in a crowded room or when other people are present. You've to learn to listen properly too. There's an old Arab proverb that says God has given us two ears and one mouth so that we can learn to listen at least twice as much as we talk."

I promised to heed the advice with, "Yes, sir."

"Even so, never let anyone tell you preaching is not important. Preach not because you have to say something, but because you have something to say. And don't serve up half a Christ."

I was not quite sure what he meant so I remained silent.

28

"I learned to preach the hard way," he said to me another day when he was on the same subject. "You know I served one of my curacies under Bishop Henn at Burnley Parish Church. He was a hard critic. I once, greatly daring, asked him what he had thought of my Sunday evening sermon. After a great deal of thought the good Bishop said, 'Two things struck me about it; first, at least you had managed to choose a good text at the beginning; and secondly, I couldn't help thinking you missed many an opportunity of bringing it to a close'." Wyatt laughed at the remembrance of the incident, and I laughed politely. He rounded off his reminiscences with, "Scored a point off him one day though when he complained that my sermon wouldn't convert a flea. I said, 'Bishop, to be perfectly honest, I'm not out to convert fleas'."

He took me to task one day about an address I had given in church the night before. "Your sermon was too technical," he grumbled, "like a page out of a theological textbook." Then he went on, "Never over-estimate the knowledge of your congregation, and never under-estimate their intelligence. And remember this too, Brown — when you mount the pulpit and look down on the faces in front of you, there will always be at least one person there with a broken heart, longing for healing and help. Make sure there is always something in what you are saying that brings the comfort of Christ to those in special need. Let me give you a text to guide your preaching throughout your ministry — Isaiah 40 verse 1: 'Comfort ye, comfort ye my people, saith your God'."

Wyatt himself was an excellent preacher, no matter how he had learned the craft, and he did try to train his curates to follow suit. I had been warned about one of his little ploys by my predecessor as curate, Victor Whitsey.

He warned me that in my second year there would be a particular challenge. "When you are in the Vestry all ready to process into the church itself, the boss will ask to see your sermon notes, as though he's making sure you have prepared properly. Then he'll put your notes into his pocket and tell you to preach extempore that evening, from the heart, and all that.''

I was grateful for the warning, and because I was so nervous in the pulpit, took the precaution of making a duplicate set of notes for my Sunday evening sermons. One set, on a postcard I used to slip into the front page of the pulpit Bible as I walked through the church on my way to the vestry; the other postcard was kept in my pocket. I was prepared to meet cunning with cunning and thus save my bacon.

Then it happened: exactly as Victor had forecasted. My notes were confiscated as Wyatt pocketed them with a sadistic smile that completely contradicted his words — ''This is hurting me more than it hurts you.'' I kept a straight face, even pretended to be somewhat crestfallen, but inwardly I was rejoicing that my extra work was about to be rewarded. I knew Wyatt would not be able to see my surreptitious use of notes for he sat underneath the pulpit with his back to it.

In the hymn before the sermon I even toyed with the idea of doing what one of Spurgeon's students had done when the great man had played a similar trick on him. He had produced the shortest sermon on record, by saying, ''My subject is Zacchaeus. He was a man of very small stature; so am I. Secondly, Zacchaeus was very much up a tree; so am I. Thirdly, Zacchaeus made haste and came down; so will I.'' And he did!

Half way through the hymn, Bill in full sail with billowing gown and silver verge on his shoulder appeared, ready to lead me to the pulpit. I stopped fantasising for I knew I would not have the guts to do the Zacchaeus thing. No need anyway, I thought, as I followed Bill's slow dignified steps to the place where I was to preach.

What a relief as I saw the postcard just sticking out of the Bible. I took a deep breath ready to begin, opening the Bible as I did so. The people were settling into their seats, lots of them, getting on for two hundred. The shuffling scraping noises died out; the special light over the pulpit was switched on from the back, and I got ready to begin.

Then horror of horrors! I saw the postcard was blank. I could not believe my eyes as I turned it this way and that. Not quite blank, I noticed, something in pencil in the bottom corner. There was no time to examine it further. The silence was getting disconcerting, my heart was pounding. Then the adrenaline, born of panic, surged through my veins and I began to speak. At first very haltingly, but I really had prepared thoroughly and some of it began to come back into my mind. Perhaps it was because I was so hyped up that I was even able to plot some kind of revenge on the Rector. I guessed that the Wardens and some of his special friends would have been let into his little secret, so in the midst of my plight I saw a small way of hitting back.

As my confidence increased a little, I picked up the blank postcard and made it appear that I was reading from it. Just looking down at it now and again was enough to give the impression I wished to convey. I was glad when it was all over, but hoped I had at least raised a question mark in the Rector's mind. No doubt his minions would give him a detailed report of my pulpit activities.

"Well done," said one or two as they went out. There was silence from Wyatt. I took the nearly-blank postcard home and showed it Joyce. After supper I examined it carefully and could just make out the pencil marking. It was a Biblical reference, hardly legible, but looking like 'Matt 6, 27'. I got out my Bible to check — I read, "Which of you by taking thought can add one cubit to his stature?" I scratched my head and wondered whether this could be one of Wyatt's wry jokes. I hoped that somebody else in a clerical household, not a hundred miles away, was also scratching his head and wondering. I resolved that if he did it to me again to make sure, I would preach the Zacchaeus sermon. That would shake him!

I was struggling for words again at one time, but on this occasion not in the pulpit. It was one of those times when I was 'on duty' at the public cemetery in the middle of the town.

Being 'on duty' meant taking the funeral service of those people who had no connection with their own church. The local clergy were listed on a rota, and found themselves officiating in turn for a week at a time for and with bereaved people they had never seen before and whom they were unlikely to see again. It was not a good system as far as pastoral care was concerned, but it prevailed at the time and had to be endured.

Mr. Jebb, the cemetery superintendent, was something of a wag, and on his appointment a year or so before had amused the management committee by thanking them for giving him the job before solemnly declaring that he hoped he would only let them all down once! I was never sure whether some of the things he said were part of his macabre sense of humour or just plain gaffes. Like the time he introduced the chief mourner at a funeral to me with the words, "Ah Mr. Brown, this is the corpse's brother."

He was a fat, bouncy little man, who liked to beam at people, and was in some ways a partial antidote to the dismal and depressing atmosphere generated by the cemetery chapel. Ill-lit, musty, inadequately heated, and not very clean, its only merit was that it made the second part of the burial service, which took place at the graveside, seem an improvement and more bearable.

On this occasion, I stood with Mr. Jebb outside the chapel door as the hearse, followed by a taxi, appeared on the scene. It was a cold December afternoon with the light already beginning to fade. I led the procession inside, reading the opening sentences — "We brought nothing into this world, and it is certain we can carry nothing out". It was as cold inside as out and my breath was coming forth like steam from an old-fashioned train.

As usual, once the coffin and the mourners were in position, the undertaker and his men quickly disappeared from the chapel — no doubt for a smoke in Mr. Jebb's office. I saw in the gloom that there was but a single mourner, an old, bent man, installed in the front pew. A quick word with him revealed his name was Albert and he was burying his wife aged 78. I did not want to embarrass him by getting too matey, but I tried to make the service as personal and friendly as possible. I was in the middle of the Bible Reading when there came an interruption — "Hang on a minute, Vicar," he called out, "I must make water — back in a jiffy." With that he disappeared through the door at the back.

I stood by the reading-desk and waited for three or four minutes until he reappeared. With an upraised hand he asked me to resume. "Carry on, my friend," he suggested. I gave a very short address, got him to join in the prayers by finding the place for him in the battered and damp Prayer Book that he was holding, and finally walked alongside him to the graveside. The coffin went to its last resting place as I said the Prayers of Committal, and then pronounced the Blessing.

I turned and held out my hand. "Goodbye," I said, "I'll get your local Vicar to pop round and see you sometime. Would you like that?"

"Worst ruddy service I've ever been to," he said, ignoring my question. He continued in the same vein. "Very disappointing, a right poor do."

I was staggered to say the least. Standing there shivering slightly from the cold I asked what was wrong with it.

"I'll tell you what was wrong with it — you've missed out the most important bit, you haven't had 'Abide with me'."

I tried to explain that that hymn was not part of the funeral service, but he was not listening. "I want that hymn," he persisted, "come on lad, sing it for me." I gave an appealing look at the undertaker standing on the other side of the grave before striking up with the well-known words. I knew from the start that I had pitched it in the wrong key, but the three or four men standing by did their best to assist with the rendering.

The struggle was not confined to the music. The makeshift choir seemed to have different opinions about the order of the verses, but we did all finish at the same time, and Albert was highly delighted that his needs — whether emotional, liturgical or spiritual — had been met. He gave me his benediction — "I hope thou lives a long, long time," he said. As he got into a taxi for the homeward run, I promised again to drop a line to his parish priest asking for a visit. I got the impression Albert was not too thrilled at the prospect!

Mr. Jebb had the book ready for me to sign when I called in the office on my way out. I saw he had put a large poster on the noticeboard which was normally used only to remind people of the fees for the various items of expenditure incurred in burials and the maintenance of graves. As I signed the book, I could see Mr. Jebb was very anxious that I should read his handiwork. In large letters it proclaimed:

CEMETERY FACELIFT
Stiff Opposition To Neglect!
Volunteer Bodies Will Be Raised To Remedy This Grave Situation.

This was vintage Jebb, even better than his similar notice the previous year, when he had written, "During the Christmas period, this cemetery will be maintained by a skeleton staff". For a man whose home as well as his job lay within the cemetery walls, a sense of humour was obviously a godsend.

I left the cemetery cold and ready for a cup of tea, but I knew I had to make an important call before I could put my feet up for a couple of hours. Joyce had asked me to collect a cat from a woman who was in the Mothers' Union. The night before Joyce had been telling her of the problem we were experiencing with mice. They were all over the place and Joyce was scared stiff. We had actually killed fifteen of them in one day, either by trapping, poisoning, or clubbing. I found it extremely distasteful, and the offer of the loan of

a wonderful cat that would end the plague came like manna
from heaven. "Our Blackie will see them off," Mrs. Harrison
had promised, "and them that escape will never come back
— she's a real tiger."

Mrs. Harrison had tied a piece of string round the cat's
collar in case I lost my grip and she bolted. I promised to
make sure she did not get out of the house unless I took her
out on the string. I listened carefully to the instructions
regarding food and drink, then with the cat's head peeping
out from my raincoat, I headed triumphantly for home. Our
troubles were as good as over. A saucer of milk and a piece
of a lamb chop left over from lunch disappeared inside the
cat with remarkable alacrity. We rejoiced that she had made
herself at home so quickly. Now she had to sing for her supper,
demonstrate her prowess, and wreak havoc among the mice
population. I carried her into the dining-room, the place
where there had been the most sightings. She curled up on
the rug in front of the fire. How clever, I thought, she would
make the mice think she was asleep, lull them into a false
sense of security, and then pounce. I closed the door and went
to have tea in the kitchen.

I always enjoyed this time of day, from about five o'clock until going out for Evensong just before seven — it was a period when I could take up my other role as a father, and play with Mark for a bit. Eventually Joyce warned me of the time. "Better be getting ready for church," she said, as she grabbed a reluctant Mark and started to get him ready for bed.

As a matter of fact, I was destined not to go to church that night at all, for as I was collecting the various toys from the floor, we had an unexpected visitor in the shape of Canon Wyatt.

He was very apologetic. "Terribly sorry to bother you, but I do need your help, Joyce," he stammered; he was never good at asking for or accepting help. He stood there with his large black Canon's Homburg in his hands, twisting it round and round with embarrassment. He refused the offer of a chair.

"No thanks, I'm in a hurry," he said, "I've actually called about Mrs. Shuttleworth, my housekeeper. She's been ill for a few days. We thought it was just a cold but she seems to be going worse and she's had to stay in bed all day. Got the doctor this morning and he's given her a bottle of medicine, but she does look a bit odd this evening, and I should be grateful, Joyce, if you would have a look at her." He knew, of course, that Joyce had been a hospital nurse before we moved into the parish.

She slipped on a coat, and together they headed for the Rectory. I took over the business of getting a child of two to bed. No sooner had I managed it than Joyce was back with a depressing tale.

Mrs. Shuttleworth was practically unconscious. The Rector had given her a cup of tea earlier in the day and she had simply let it fall out of her hands as soon as he was out of the room. She had also become incontinent. It had been necessary to change not only the sheets and blankets, but the mattress as well. Canon Wyatt had helped her as best he could. Now she was home simply to collect a few things before returning to spend the night by the bedside. The doctor had been

36

summoned again and had given his opinion that the housekeeper was too ill with pneumonia to be moved to hospital.

I awoke at seven to see Joyce moving around the bedroom. She looked tired after her vigil. The old lady had died an hour before. "I've laid her out and sent for an undertaker," she explained. "I understand she hasn't many relatives but the Rector's telephoning them now. The funeral will probably be early next week." When it came it was a simple, quiet affair, with only a few of us to pay our last respects.

With hindsight, this sad little episode was not without significance. For one thing, it was the first of many occasions when Joyce went out to use her nursing skills and experience on a voluntary basis in the community. This was not from a sense of obligation, but a ready response to a particular need, bringing with it a deep satisfaction in using training and talents for the benefit of others. One of John Wesley's prayers was, "O Lord, let me not live to be useless," and to feel useful and valued is a human need bringing a special sense of fulfilment and joy.

Because of this incident I was alerted to the fact that many other people did the same kind of thing, that is gave their time and talents for the sake of others. Largely unheralded, often taken for granted, there was a surprising amount of good neighbourliness in the parish. I could not pretend it all sprang from church membership, but a lot of it did, and from this I took heart. You cannot read the Gospels without seeing that Jesus did not tell people how to be good in the manner of a moral teacher. He told them how to be happy and He had an incredible recipe for this, a complete reversal of worldly wisdom. If you want to find your life you must first lose it. The opportunities are boundless, and God's love is experienced not only in what He gives but also in what He asks: in both He is profligate.

"Every act of kindness is a little death" wrote William Blake, but he speaks of the death of self which brings freedom and new life. How beautifully this has been expressed by James Montgomery in his poem on the Good Samaritan:

Stript, wounded, beaten nigh to death,
I found him by the highway side.
I roused his pulse, brought back his breath,
Revived his spirit, and supplied
Wine, oil, refreshment: he was healed:
I had myself a wound concealed;
But from that hour forgot the smart
And peace bound up my broken heart.

Alas, Blackie the cat had brought little happiness into my situation and I returned her at the earliest opportunity — on my way to Mattins, in fact. Blackie had failed dismally to live up to her glittering reputation. I was glad to tuck her under my raincoat once more and hand her over, complete with string, to the good Mrs. Harrison. In my spiel of thanks, I said I thought she might have done something to frighten the mice away. I was actually much more sure of what I did not say, namely, that she had shredded a settee cushion; had been seen sleeping while two mice played a game of tig not an inch from her whiskers; and that in spite of my best endeavours, there had been serious lavatorial problems. When to all this was added the spate of meowing that had got me out of bed at three in the morning, the discharge with ignominy from ecclesiastical service was inevitable. The only bright spot came with the realisation that by comparison, the mice problem seemed less important after Blackie's departure. The cure can indeed sometimes be worse than the disease.

Relieved of the animal, I headed with a light step towards the church. I liked to be early for the daily services since Canon Wyatt had the curious habit of starting them ten minutes early, whether I was there or not. But as well as that, it was not uncommon for people to use those occasions to make contact with the clergy. This was the case one Spring morning when I discovered one of the local undertakers waiting for me in the church porch.

"Do wish you curates were on the phone," he complained. "Knew I could get hold of you here at this time. Have you got your diary with you?"

I took it out and turned the pages, and then agreed a convenient date and time for a funeral.

"I wonder why they've asked for me," I said. "The address is outside the parish and the name doesn't ring a bell. Mr. Jenkins did you say?"

"Yes, Jenkins, Albert Jenkins, lived the other side of town. It was in his Will apparently that you were to officiate. He's no relatives, all being done through his solicitor. By the way, he also requested that you should sing 'Abide with me' at the graveside. Didn't know you were gifted in that respect, Mr. Brown," he said with a false innocence.

The penny dropped. We both laughed. I said, "Now I've a request. Please make sure you bring half a dozen hymn books with you, and select from among your staff those blokes with a bit of tune in them, OK? Oh yes, and a tuning-fork too, if you don't mind."

I went in to Mattins, and at the end said a special prayer for Albert, that he might rest in peace. I knew we would carry out his wishes as best we could.

It was easy to know what to say for Albert. I made it a 'proxy prayer', using the words of 'Abide with me', of course. The last verse particularly seemed appropriate:

Hold thou thy Cross before my closing eyes;
Shine through the gloom, and point me to the skies:
Heaven's morning breaks, and earth's vain shadows
   flee;
In life, in death, O Lord, abide with me.

As I walked down the aisle on my way out, I was wondering why on earth it was the 'Cup-Final Hymn'. Perhaps be better if they dropped it at Wembley, maybe it would not seem quite so hackneyed then. If taken seriously, the words certainly made a powerful devotional prayer. As I got to the door, another line from the hymn came into mind: "Change and decay in all around I see." Bit morbid, I thought, but I knew change was on the way for me, if not decay! The Bishop had told me recently he thought my four years in the parish were enough. "It's time to move on when the right job appears," he had said.

Bill was in the porch using a broom as I went out. The weather was the subject of his final comments that morning. "T'was white o'er first thing, then it rained stair-rods, and now t'sun is trying to get out. Thou never knows what's coming next, does ta?"

"You can say that again, Bill," I replied with much feeling. I felt he had spoken more wisely than he knew. I hurried down the road ready for breakfast.

CHAPTER THREE

"A man he was to all the country dear,
And passing rich on forty pounds a year."
(The Country Parson: Oliver Goldsmith, 1728-1774)

I came down the wide, uncarpeted stairs feeling absolutely
frozen with teeth chattering, shivering from head to foot. I
rubbed my hands together vigorously and slapped myself
across the chest in an attempt to generate enough heat to ward
off hypothermia.

Apart from an igloo in the polar regions, I could not imagine
many colder dwelling places than this. Not that it looked like
an igloo, more like a manor-house, built as it was of stone
and with generous proportions.

We had just spent the first night in our new home and could
have chosen any one of the six bedrooms in which to put our
bed. Two of the rooms could easily have taken three or four
double beds, but we had opted for a smaller one in the interests
of warmth and comfort. Hope springs eternal in the human
breast!

The cold was bad enough, but made worse by the look and
smell of dampness everywhere. Not surprising really, for the
house had been empty for the best part of a year. However,
we had very much wanted to come here so were not too
daunted by the dank conditions.

I moved into the hall and picked up the solitary letter that
had been pushed through the letter-box. My spirits rose as
I looked at it, for there in black and white was my new status.
After my name, came "St. John's Vicarage". I was now a
Vicar, or at least soon would be, for the Induction Service
to be taken by the Bishop was fixed for a couple of days hence.

The thought of being my own boss brought great

pleasure and now I would have my own church and parish. It had been a long haul for I had been training for this for about nine years, what with time at University, Theological College, and in a Curacy. This had been my one hope and ambition from the age of seven, more than twenty years before. "Yippee!" The temperature might be low but my spirits were high.

Deciding it was too cold to fiddle about reading correspondence at that moment, I put the letter into my overcoat pocket. Having gone upstairs wearing a top-coat, it was easy to come down similarly attired. That pocket preserved my peace of mind a little while longer, for if the outside of the envelope had brought pleasure, the same alas could not be said of the inside. Blissfully unaware that a crisis was brewing, I pulled the thick woollen scarf tighter round my neck, moved down a long corridor to the back door and went out into the January morning to chop wood for a fire.

The stone sets in the yard had been laid to stop the horses slipping on days exactly like this. Before letting them do me similar service, I stood at the top of the steps looking with appreciation at the attractive scene that met my eyes. The heavy frost had sprayed the buildings here and there with diamond clusters, and the pristine white shawl worn by the trees was ethereal and delicate. The silence could almost be felt.

I looked to the left across the thirty-yard divide to the impressive stone church with its powerful tower and large gothic windows. On the other side of the Vicarage could be seen the Church School, its several buildings, new and old, grouped together in the middle of the playground. I took it all in, liking what I saw, excited at the prospect of being involved in those things the buildings brought to mind.

I braved the early morning air and stepped out for the stables. I had noticed a stack of wood there suitable for chopping. Thirty or more years had elapsed since the Vicar of those days had used the stables for their original purpose.

The vehicle the horses had pulled was presumably housed next door in what was still called the coach-house.

Those were the days, I mused, as I swung the axe and produced a supply of kindling wood. I decided I did not want them back. I was not too sure how a priest with three or four servants and with all the other trappings of privilege could bridge the gap with the vast majority of his mainly poor parishioners. At least, I would not have to face that problem. And in any case, I preferred a bike to a horse; a lot less bother, I suspected, with no need to feed or mollycoddle, to say nothing of vet's fees. With a bucket of coal in each hand and sticks on top of both, I hurried inside to light the kitchen fire.

By this time Joyce was downstairs. She had deposited Mark in his baby-chair while she prepared breakfast. He looked like a little pixie, dressed in a red knitted-suit complete with a pom-pom hat pulled down over his ears. For good value, my college scarf went round him diagonally and was tied at the back. He looked snug and warm with his cheeks matching his suit.

"Don't tell me you have to light the fires in this great house, Sir," Joyce mocked. "I thought all Sir had to do was pull one of those bells that I see in every room."

"It's the butler's day off," I retorted, "and the footman's joined the Foreign Legion. But to be serious, I'm only too relieved that the cold-water tap is still running. Thought it might have frozen up again, like when we arrived."

Soon the fire was roaring away, and I concluded that the draughts in the kitchen did, at least, help in that respect. I tried to cut them off with rolled newspapers stuffed under the three doors when they had outlived their usefulness as bellows. As the kitchen warmed up, the smell of toast pervaded the air, and the three of us huddled round the grate, enjoying food and drink at the beginning of a new day in our new home. The dull red bars of the small electric fire in the background did not seem so inadequate now.

It was easy to see that Joyce was as excited by it all as

I was. "I'm sure we can make it comfortable in time," she said, "it's a lovely old place, and I've got a feeling we're going to be very happy here." We fell silent as we enjoyed the warmth, and savoured the prospect of contented and interesting days ahead. Even the chilling fears that came from the knowledge of my own inadequacies, coupled with the well-nigh impossible task of meeting the high expectations of my new parishioners, melted away, and there was peace.

But not for long. It was shattered by the telephone bell echoing through the house. Brreeng-brreeng, brreeng-brreeng; I rushed to the one phone that had so many extension bells. It was in the study. For the first time I was able to announce into the mouthpiece, "St. John's Vicarage."

"Mr. Brown?" asked a woman's voice. "Oh good. This is Miss Peto, Miss Betty Peto, at Leyland Vicarage. My father has asked me to ring with the message that he hopes to be present, God willing, at your Induction Service on Thursday evening. He is prepared to accede to the Bishop's request and to make the Presentation."

I tried to keep the surprise out of my voice as I replied, "Oh good, I'm so glad. Do please give him my good wishes and tell him how much I shall look forward to seeing him again."

"Thank you," Miss Peto said, "I'm pleased about it too. He had a letter from the Bishop this morning — that's what has led to this decision."

As soon as our goodbyes were said I could not get to the kitchen quick enough to give Joyce the news. She found it difficult to believe. "You're pulling my leg, aren't you," she suggested. She took a lot of convincing, but finally she believed me. "I can only think he's sucking up to the Bishop," she said. "Maybe he wants to be a big-gun, you know, a Canon."

Instead of sitting by the fire again, a very tempting prospect, I grabbed a duster and made for the study. There was work to be done. Two tea-chests and half-a-dozen cardboard boxes

44

contained books which had to be unpacked and placed on the shelves that covered the whole of one wall from floor to ceiling.

A flick of the duster and a quick decision about its place on the shelves, was the method I employed. It was a fairly mechanical process giving me the opportunity to think of other things as I got on with the task. The recent phone call dominated my thoughts.

The Reverend Laurence Peto was the long-standing Vicar of Leyland, having been there for more than eighteen years. This ancient church had, for hundreds of years, been the centre of a very large parish. In the course of time, with the great increase in the population, which came mainly in the 19th century, it had been necessary to create four new parishes out of this same area, one of which was my own parish of Whittle-le-Woods. All this had happened well over a hundred years ago but the link with the old mother church was maintained by the patronage system. This meant that the Vicar of Leyland always had the right to appoint the Vicars of the daughter parishes.

Not surprising then that Mr. Peto intended to be present in two days' time to present me to the Bishop at the Induction Service? Well, there's the rub, for he had in fact refused to appoint me and, more than that, had tried to persuade several other priests to take on the job instead. It was even rumoured that he had been heard to declaim that, ''Brown will only go there over my dead body.''

I smiled wryly as I dusted another book and pushed it into place. I was remembering my interview with the old man some eight months before. I had arrived at his Vicarage feeling very nervous indeed, and had popped into his church for a quick morale-boosting prayer. The tension stemmed from the fact that I wanted the job as Vicar of Whittle very much indeed. I also knew Mr. Peto was considered somewhat eccentric and I was not quite sure what to expect. Eventually I rang his door-bell, determined if possible to make a good impression but, alas, this I signally failed to do.

He was in his late seventies at the time of our meeting. A shock of unruly snow-white hair showed to advantage the quite handsome face beneath. A slightly aquiline nose, a square jaw, piercing blue eyes, and a more or less permanent smile, made him appear a strong but benign figure. Tall at one time, he was now stooped and slightly ungainly, but still he retained a natural dignity. Everybody who knew him recognised his deep sincerity and good intentions, but not even his best friend would have denied that he was a bit of an oddball.

He ushered me into his rather gloomy booklined study and got me ensconced in a deep leather armchair. He took a similar chair on the other side of the fireplace; the gas-fire hissed gently between us. The interview, which was to last more than an hour, began with a long rambling extempore prayer, the main purpose of which seemed to be to ensure that God knew the purpose of the interview and the issues involved. I suspected that some of it might have been slightly superfluous!

Then came the first of Mr. Peto's three questions, each of which, sadly, I seemed to muff. "Tell me, Mr. Brown," he said in a soft deep voice, "tell me the date and the circumstances when you first took the Lord Jesus Christ into your life as your personal saviour."

I had not expected to open the batting facing a bouncer. I played a defensive shot. "I cannot do that," I replied, "for I have not had a Damascus-Road-type conversion. My parents were good church people who brought up their five children to go to church and to believe in God. I was a choirboy at seven, confirmed at fourteen, and a Sunday School teacher at sixteen. My faith has had its ups and downs, and once or twice nearly disappeared, but gradually it has matured and strengthened. And you will appreciate, I've had to think it out carefully before I've reached this stage in my life."

"Um, um, ah, ah," said the old man, and I could see from his face that he was not at all happy with my spiritual biography. He screwed up his eyes and looked intently into mine as though he were trying to make windows into my soul.

I interrupted the long silence by having another go. "Surely Mr. Peto, one of the things that should be said about conversion is that it is not less real because it is gradual. It may not be a sudden miracle, but it can be just as great a miracle. There is a line in Browning that reminds us that we can see the miraculous not only 'in the comet's rush, but in the rose's birth'." I looked across to see if I was making any impression. Mr. Peto's eyes were now on the ceiling. I felt I ought to underline the point I was trying to make. "I'm with you in the sense that even though conversion may be gradual, there ought to be a time when the growing Christian realises what has happened and accepts Christ's forgiveness, love and friendship. You know, establishes a personal relationship with Him in prayer, Sacrament, and Bible reading. And, of course, he needs to dedicate his life to Him again and again. When I was confirmed, Mr. Peto, my Vicar taught me a little prayer which I still use every time I receive Holy Communion. I say, 'Jesu my Lord, I Thee adore: O make me love Thee more and more'. It's true I can't name the day of my conversion, but some things are gradual, like the morning following the night. Many Christians find it impossible to say exactly ..."

I was stopped mid-sentence with a quotation from St. John's Gospel. The voice now was much louder. "Jesus said, 'Except a man be born again, he cannot see the Kingdom of God'."

I retaliated with an aphorism that may have helped my argument but which did little to advance my hopes of the job I was seeking. "Mr. Peto," I said slowly and deliberately, "I don't need to know my date of birth to know that I'm alive."

"That's not a quotation from Holy Writ, is it?" he said in a disapproving tone. "It's the Bible, not Browning or anybody else, that counts with me. But never mind, let's move on."

I waited for the next salvo. He cleared his throat, fixed me again with his intense stare, and asked, "What do you think of Thomas Cheyne's book on Isaiah?"

Never having heard of Mr. Cheyne I was able to indicate quite truthfully that the book had made no noticeable contribution to my theological education. I tried to soften the answer with, "I've so much reading to catch up with, but I intend to make study an important part of my ministry, and I shall certainly remember your commendation of Mr. Cheyne."

Maybe if I had left it at that it would have been better, but I tried to underline the sincerity of my resolve by adding, "What is the title of the book, and when was it published?"

He answered by pulling himself very laboriously out of his chair and walking shakily across the room to the book shelves. He straightened himself as best he could, reached up on tiptoe, and took down a thick dusty volume from a shelf above his head. He opened it fully in the middle before closing it with a bang. A cloud of dust emerged. Then, blowing more dust from the edges, he opened it at the beginning and read the title page: "The Prophecies of Isaiah, by Thomas K. Cheyne, 1870." Sadness permeated his voice which was little more than a whisper as he said, "I am surprised, nay astonished, that you do not know this great book. Whatever is the Church coming to!"

Mr. Cheyne was placed on the desk while he made another sortie to the bookshelves. "Now, what about this one?" he exclaimed, turning round with another great tome in his arms.

I groaned almost audibly as I faced the next question in the same field. He was waving the book up and down, holding it with both hands, as he said, "This is J. F. McFadyen, entitled, 'A Dictionary of Christ and the Gospels'. You will know this, of course?"

I was spared from an immediate answer by a tap on the door. It opened and Miss Peto came into the study bearing a tray on which stood a steaming pot of coffee, cups and saucers, and a plate of chocolate biscuits. I knew at that moment what the beleaguered garrison at Mafeking must have felt like when they heard the bugle-sound of the British Army outside the city.

"Coffee, father," she announced, and placed the tray on a side-table near the door.

"Thank you, my dear, thank you," acknowledged the old man, and before the door was fully closed behind her he resumed his tirade on the books that every Christian pastor should have read. Stumbling across the room once more, he dragged a chair into position and managed to scramble on to it, kneeling before dragging himself to an upright position. He was obviously bent on getting at the volumes on the top shelf. He swayed about dangerously as though drunk.

I feared for his safety, getting up at once and going to his aid. I held the back of the chair with one hand and supported his back with the other. "Take this," he said, handing me a book, "and this ... and this." I helped him down to the floor, to safety and comparative stability.

Cheyne and McFadyen were joined on the desk by the others, and Mr. Peto lumbered over to explain his selection and continue with the inquisition. I decided to try to forestall him. "The coffee, Mr. Peto," I said hoarsely, for the dust and even more the tension had dried my throat. "The coffee," I repeated, pointing to the tray near the door.

Still standing by the books, he looked quite pained as he raised his right hand and pointed a finger to heaven. "There are more important things in life than coffee, Mr. Brown," he said reprovingly and then, as though announcing a text from the pulpit he proclaimed, "Man shall not live by bread alone, but by every word that proceedeth out of the mouth of God."

"Quite so," I groaned, resigning myself to a further period of unease. The delicious aroma of the coffee floated across the room to intensify my longing. That was the nearest I came to tasting it that morning.

At any rate, the interruption had stopped his train of thought and he left the desk and dropped into the easy-chair once more. He moved onto the third main question. It took the form of a proposition. "You know, I expect, that Jesus Christ visited this country when He was a young man, eh? eh?" He sat back waiting for a reply.

Not really knowing what to say I answered with a quotation from William Blake. "'And did those feet in ancient time, walk upon England's mountains green?' Yes, I know there is a legend to that effect."

The old man exploded with indignation — "A legend! A legend! There is a very well-founded tradition that, in my opinion, puts it beyond doubt. But never mind, never mind," he said with a degree of finality that suggested the last straw had been placed on the camel's back. "Never mind, never mind, let's go and have some lunch." He gave a deep sigh of disappointment as he lumbered to his feet.

This was the first time lunch had been mentioned. I had been hoping to escape immediately the interview ended for I did find him very wearing but I was now shepherded into the dining-room. I stood with Vicar and daughter waiting for grace to be said. In fact it was sung. The two of them blending harmoniously with words and tune new to me. Mr. Peto glanced in my direction half-way through, disappointed no doubt, that his guest was as ignorant of the grace as he was of Mr. Cheyne and Mr. McFadyen.

The simple meal was taken largely in silence and at the end I beat a hasty retreat. Mr. Peto saw me to the door. He explained that he felt unable to reach a decision at that moment but that he would give the matter his prayerful and careful consideration. "I will be in touch with you shortly," he said as I offered a word of thanks and bade him goodbye.

It was with a heavy heart that I headed for home. Even allowing for the fact that the old boy was stranger than I had expected, I felt I had handled it rather badly and blown my chance of getting the job I really wanted.

Mr. Peto never did get in touch with me. I expect he forgot what he had actually said. I waited for the postman every morning for a couple of weeks, hoping that maybe by some strange chance, he would have second thoughts. I heard on the grapevine that both the Bishop and the Archdeacon had sent him good references and recommended my appointment. But eventually, as the days went by, I knew this was wishful thinking and I gave up all hope of the job — a view confirmed when I learned that other clergymen were being sent to meet the Churchwardens and to inspect the church, the house and the parish. I resigned myself to the fact that my future ministry would probably lie elsewhere.

However, that was to underestimate the strength of opinion and the resourcefulness of the leading church folk in the parish. They had got to know me rather well by this time, for I was serving my curacy in an adjoining parish, and by agreement with my Rector, it had been arranged that I should take a service for them every other Sunday as well as spend one full day a week visiting in the parish.

Working on the principle, I suspect, that "the devil you know is better than the devil you don't", some of them started to suggest that I should be their next Vicar. That was, in fact, how the idea had first come to me. It made a strong appeal. Not to put too fine a point on it, I genuinely thought that God might well be calling me to serve in that place. I felt at home there, got on well with the people I met, and even more importantly, saw some of the things that in my opinion could be done to strengthen the work there. There were no great inspirational moments, no messages on the hot-line direct from the Almighty, but I was aware of the 'still small voice' that spoke from the application of common-sense to the salient factors in the situation. In addition, I listened to family and friends, for I have never doubted the soundness of Robert Browning's advice:

"Hush, I pray you!
What if this friend happens to be — God?"

If the local people were to get the priest they wanted, it was obviously necessary to thwart Mr. Peto's intention of appointing someone else. The methods used were crude but effective. He sent in all half-a-dozen evangelical clergymen who had presumably passed the test I failed. At intervals of about a month, these poor chaps came to meet the Standing Committee and to be shown round the place.

Dick Chaplin, a committee member, was a cobbler by profession whose little wooden shop lay immediately across the road from the Vicarage. His house was twenty yards behind the shop on rising ground. It was natural that he should be given the task of having the keys available for those who came to see church and house.

He had a marvellous vantage point, able to see every person and vehicle that came within a hundred yards of the church site. He was a small, cheerful, busy man who loved every minute of the intrigue in which he and half-a-dozen others found themselves engaged.

At the time, I knew little or nothing of what was going on and it was, in fact, at the Reception following my Induction that Dick made his confession and revealed all. Roaring with laughter, he said, "Whenever we were asked to show anybody round the Vicarage, I would go across an hour or so before to prepare the ground or, more accurately, prepare the walls! I used a watering-can, sprinkling the best part of a gallon of water in every one of the bedrooms, from ceiling to floor."

More laughter followed as I heard how the committee members conducted the next stage in the operation when they were in the Vicarage with the prospective Vicar and his wife. "Not fit to live in, this place," Reg, a Churchwarden, would say as he pointed out the dampness. It was the church Treasurer, who made the next contribution. "If you've plenty of money to pay for the repairs here, this is the place for you. Unfortunately, the parish wouldn't be able to help much towards the cost for we are nearly broke."

The other Churchwarden, also Reg, was now expected to add a few dark brushstrokes. "Don't know how the last Vicar survived. Mind, he and his wife were always ill, never free from colds. This place doesn't seem to dry out properly even in the summer."

Then it was back to the other Warden once more. Apparently, he kept his best lines until the end and they were spoken with as much sadness as he could muster. "I think it's the dampness that attracts the rats. I've heard that some of them are nearly as big as young cats." His voice dropped to a whisper as new depths were plumbed: "Of course, it may be the drains that attract them, for there is obviously something seriously wrong with a system that produces those terrible smells in the house from time to time."

At this point, six clergymen in succession, together with their wives, seemed to lose some of the enthusiasm for the parish, and remembered other appointments that necessitated their speedy withdrawal from the scene. It worked like clockwork every time, though there was one bad moment when one of the prospective Vicars returned unexpectedly with a friend who was a surveyor. Dick spotted their arrival and used his initiative. Quickly he briefed his co-operative wife. When the two men arrived for the keys they were invited in for a cup of tea. "My husband is busy at the moment, but he'll be back soon with the keys."

Not a word of a lie. Dick was busy, very busy, preparing the premises in the usual way. The skulduggery even fooled the professional who said afterwards that he had obtained some of the highest damp-readings on his instruments that he had ever known. His opinion was that the stone must be extremely porous or, maybe, the gutters were backing up. Soon that clergyman, like the others, went out of the reckoning, and the local conspirators breathed a sigh of relief once more.

Eventually came the great day when smiles of satisfaction adorned their faces for they knew they had reached an important landmark. Six months had then elapsed since the vacancy occurred. Eureka! This was what they had been working for. Church law laid it down that if a vacancy had not been filled in that period of time, the right to appoint a Vicar moved from the patron to the Bishop. The very day this happened, I was summoned to the Bishop's house for tea, and between the salmon sandwiches and buttered scones, was formally offered the Living of Whittle-le-Woods. I accepted there and then with much pleasure, and on the way home on the bus had the opportunity to reflect that "God moves in a mysterious way His wonders to perform". I did not realise at the time that He had been given so much local help!

The balloon went up twenty-four hours after my appointment was announced. Mr Peto had apparently been in touch with the press. The local newspapers made a meal of it, one of them carrying the headline, "Curate 'Passed Over' Becomes Vicar". Even the nationals carried the story, with the Daily Mail giving it quite a bit of space under the heading, "Vicar Dispute — Bishop made Choice". Mr. Peto had said to their reporter that, "What it means is that the patron does not count for anything if the Churchwardens don't agree with him." He lamented the fact that he had sent six candidates who had not been acceptable to the church council and he equivocated somewhat by saying, "My main reason for rejecting Mr. Brown was that he is clearly much too young for this position.''

The fuss soon died down and in the course of time the removal van conveyed our goods and chattels two miles along the road to our new home. Unpacking our meagre belongings was no problem, but getting water for a cup of tea was, and success only came when I had used a blow-lamp to thaw out the frozen pipes. After twenty-four hours all that remained to be done was the sorting out of the cases, the boxes, and the tea-chests; the kind of thing I was engaged in at that very time.

The long reverie in my new study was interrupted by a voice from the kitchen echoing down the corridors — ''Coffee, coffee, come and get it.'' For one awful moment I imagined I was back in Mr. Peto's study, but as that mirage faded I was cheered by the realisation that this was coffee to be tasted, not dangled as an object of torture: ''twas a consummation devoutly to be wished for'', and I hurried to the kitchen.

The place looked surprisingly shipshape: Joyce certainly knew how to get a move on. The many cardboard boxes had gone and pots and pans were stowed away on shelves and in cupboards. Curtains and cushions were in place, a home-made rug was on the floor, and with the colour and the warmth it looked homely and inviting. Mark was in his play-pen stationed in front of the roaring fire.

As we enjoyed our coffee, we again reflected on the surprising news of Mr. Peto's *volte-face*. Joyce was full of admiration for the way the Bishop had worked the oracle. ''Obviously he has been pouring oil on troubled waters, wanting you to begin your ministry here with the minimum of bother.''

''Sure,'' I replied, ''and I know there are some folk in the parish, not many, but some, who share Mr. Peto's churchmanship. I don't want to be at loggerheads with them, so I'm all for this public reconciliation. I might even be able to get pally with the old boy himself, later on.''

"The Bishop's letter must have been very persuasive," added Joyce, "funny he didn't send you a copy. Was there no mail today?"

For the first time, I remembered the letter I had stuffed in a pocket. I fished it out and smoothed the envelope on the table before opening it. "Glad you've reminded me, there was a letter. Here it is — postmark 'Blackburn', so it's probably from the Bishop."

It was not. It came from the Diocesan Registrar and it was as brief as it was devastating. "I enclose my account for drawing up the Deed of Institution and for completing the other legal requirements in connection with your Induction which is to take place later this week. The total charge of £15 should be paid before the date of the Service and I shall expect a remittance by return of post."

I read the ultimatum aloud and we both gasped. We were literally stunned. Eventually I said, "We needed that like a moose needs a hatrack." Joyce did not think that at all funny. She could face practically anything except the prospect of debt, and her fears in this area were almost pathological. "How much have we got?" I asked.

For answer she got up and went to her coat hanging behind the kitchen door. She extracted her purse from a pocket and moved to the table where I was sitting. She pulled at the press-stud and emptied the contents onto the surface in front of me. "There you have our total assets," she said, "three shillings, seven pence." Her face had gone quite pale.

I tried to cheer her up. "We'll get the 'Sequestration Fund' in a few weeks," I said, "that's the money that's gone into the stipend account since the last Vicar left, but the Wardens have to use it first to pay all the expenses for the Services during the vacancy, and various other things. Even the cost of the refreshments after the Induction comes out of it but, sooner or later, the balance will come our way. That's when we should be able to buy a carpet and some new curtains. For goodness sake, don't worry."

"That doesn't solve the immediate problem," she said with a wan smile, "and the position is even worse than you think for we've very little food in the house. I have to go now for some basic things like bread, tea, milk, and so on. Three-and-seven isn't going to go far, is it?"

She came back with fourpence!

By this time I had decided what to do. "The answer is simple," I assured Joyce, "I'll borrow the money from Fred so calm down." Fred was a brother who lived nine miles away in Preston.

"That's the only thing we can do," she agreed, "but there's just one big snag."

"I know, you mean we haven't the bus fare to Preston, don't you. Well, we have fourpence, so let's have a search for two more pennies, surely we'll find something in our pockets and your handbags."

I was wrong. Not a cent anywhere. We had a sandwich for lunch feeling a bit frustrated. Halfway through, Joyce sprang to her feet. "Got it," she said, as she hurried into the butler's pantry. "Hurrah, hurrah," I heard, as she made her way back. "We've cracked it," she said between smiles as she reappeared. In each hand was an empty Tizer bottle. "There's a penny deposit on each, we're in business. I suddenly remembered having seen them in the wine-rack. Get yourself ready while I take them back to the shop."

Half an hour later I was on the bus. Another hour and it was all settled. The money would be sent direct from Preston by money-order. It would arrive in time to beat the deadline. I returned in triumph with ten pounds in cash to tide us over for a week or two until the cash-flow problem was resolved.

We enjoyed Lancashire hot-pot for supper, once again getting as close as possible to the kitchen fire. Joyce had been busy in my absence and the place looked very different. Mark's cot now stood in one corner and a single bed in the other. "What's all this?" I enquired.

"I would have thought it was pretty obvious — hasn't the

57

penny dropped yet?''

"You are going to sleep with Mark in the kitchen tonight?''
I guessed.

"Nearly right,'' she replied, "but as a matter of fact I
suggest we all sleep here. The bed is for you; I'll sleep on
the sofa. We'll make the fire up before we get down for the
night, and I reckon we should be reasonably comfortable. I
can't face sleeping upstairs again until it gets warmer. When
I went up for the bed I saw there are actually icicles hanging
from the ceiling above the window. See what a good wife
you've got, looking after you like this.''

"Good idea,'' I said, "I'll try anything once, and this is
one way we can avoid getting pneumonia.'' As things turned
out, I was too sanguine, for that is exactly what happened
before the month was out. Mark was the victim, in spite of
our efforts, but his serious illness lay in the future as we got
settled into the house as best we could, and prepared ourselves
for the important service that was now so near.

According to the newspaper accounts, there were more than
seven hundred people present for the Induction, and
everything went smoothly. Mr. Peto behaved impeccably,
taking my right hand in his at the beginning of the ceremony
as he led me to the Bishop seated in his chair on top of the
Chancel steps. As the processional hymn died away, he cleared
his throat, and in as loud a voice as he could muster said his
piece. "Right Reverend Father in God, as the patron of this
Benefice I present unto your Lordship, Ronald Brown, Clerk
in Holy Orders, to receive at your hands Institution into the
cure of souls of this parish within your Diocese and
jurisdiction.'' By the conviction in his voice and the warmth
of his smile, I got the impression he was anxious to make it
clear that this was not a shot-gun affair.

He bowed low to the Bishop before taking his place in the
front pew with his daughter on one side, and Joyce and Mark
on the other. The Service proceeded in its usual impressive
way. Before long, I was escorted to the principal parts of the

church and at each, reminded of my pastoral and priestly duties. At the Font, the Chancel step, the Pulpit, Prayer Desk, Lectern and Altar, I was charged by the Bishop to be diligent in those things associated with those places. "I will so do, the Lord being my helper," was my response.

The Bishop was in sparkling form. In the Pulpit he took as his text words from I Timothy that had a bearing on the controversy surrounding my appointment. "Let no man despise thy youth", he thundered, looking first at me and then at the occupant of the front pew. "Too young to be a Vicar? Rubbish! In my twenties I was a lieutenant-colonel commanding a battalion during the Great War. Fifteen times I took that battalion over the top. Some people would have said that a man aged twenty-three commanding so many soldiers was ridiculous, but I don't think the troops thought that."

The Bishop made the most of the obvious analogy the occasion afforded: "We are out on a great adventure, we need men to go over the top and carry the Gospel into the dark places of the earth; to go forth in the Name of Jesus and conquer vice, wickedness, carelessness and indifference here at home."

The Bishop swung round in the Pulpit and faced me as I sat in my new stall as Incumbent. He raised his hand and pointed a finger directly at me. "Over the top, Ronald Brown, over into enemy territory, with your Christian soldiers behind you, into danger, difficulty and self-sacrifice, for that's where the Cross is, and it is in your Calvaries that you will find the Christ. You will find the One who redeemed the world at thirty-three years of age. Let no man despise thy youth!"

It was all stirring stuff. I glanced at the front pew to see how it was being received. The old man's head was on his chest and he was breathing heavily. He looked at least very relaxed! The organ introduction for the final hymn roused him. Appropriately, but accidentally, I had chosen:

Soldiers of the Cross, arise!
Gird you with your armour bright;
Mighty are your enemies,
Hard the battle ye must fight.

It was one of the other verses that seemed to challenge me most. I could more easily sing about fighting and struggling when it was couched in general terms, but this verse was rather more specific, and not for the first time that evening I felt uneasy and experienced a few qualms:

Guard the helpless; seek the stray'd;
Comfort troubles, banish grief;
In the might of God array'd,
Scatter sin and unbelief.

I was wondering whether I was up to it as I went to the Sanctuary to receive the Offertory. At close quarters, I saw the Bishop was covered in perspiration. He had obviously put a lot of effort into his address. I handed him his pastoral staff and he pronounced the Blessing.

We processed out to some lively organ music, and I caught Joyce's eye as I passed. She gave me a broad wink and wriggled her nose in her own special way. It was code, and meant that she was highly amused at something. I knew it would be some time before she would have the opportunity to share the joke.

But eventually, after more than an hour, that time came. The party really was over. The trestle-tables loaded with food had been emptied by the multitude; flowery speeches had been made welcoming us to the parish; and a splendid bouquet of red roses had been handed to Joyce, described as "the new Vicar's delightful lady wife".

Mark had been taken home straight after the Service, and the weary Bishop had stayed but a few minutes longer. Now it was our turn to walk from the almost deserted school to the Vicarage. The last of the coaches that had brought people from Chorley and other places was just driving away. We stopped in the street and waved goodbye.

"How do you feel?" asked Joyce as we turned into the Vicarage drive.

"A mixture of things," I answered, "excited, grateful it's gone so well and, most of all, relieved that it's all over. How about you?"

"I've enjoyed it, but it's good to get it behind us, isn't it? Nice folk here; they've gone out of their way to make us feel welcome. Worked hard too to produce all that lovely food. Did you eat much?"

"Not a thing, I was too busy talking to the folk. And in any case, I prefer to eat at home. Let's have some toast."

We were still sleeping in the kitchen. The baby-sitter had made up the fire, and we relaxed in front of it for a while, supper on our laps. Then, finally, we got into our beds. It was minutes later that the laughter started to come from Joyce, gently at first, but then with increasing heartiness. Soon she had to sit up in bed to catch her breath. Tears were streaming down her face.

"Come on," I said, "spill it out, what's the joke?"

With difficulty and several interruptions of laughter, she started to explain. "I was just thinking of all the palaver; do you think they would want the roses back if they saw the Reverend Vicar and his delightful lady wife sleeping rough like this?" Again she dissolved in mirth. "Do you think they would have had a whip-round if they had known we are so short of blankets that you have to top off with your overcoat?"

I joined in the laughter, infectious as it was, and for a while neither of us could say a word. By the time the silliness left us, the tension of the day had largely gone. We lay quietly in the firelight and I remembered I had something to ask her.

"What did you find so amusing at the end of the Service tonight? What with a wink and a nose wriggle, you certainly gave me the full treatment."

"Oh that; well, I suddenly had an idea. I expect it was sitting

61

with the Petos that triggered it. (By the way, I liked them both, they're going to call on us soon.) But back to my idea. You know we've been discussing names for the new baby. I know it's six months off but I had a flash of inspiration. I thought, if it's a boy, we should call him Cheyne McFadyen Brown, after your favourite authors, of course.''

"Of course. And if it's a girl?''

"How about, Tizer? Miss Tizer Brown, the one who brings refreshment in a solution!''

"Gosh, that's a bit tortuous, isn't it? But won't it be good to get to the summer with its warmer days. Surely we'll not be dossing down here in the kitchen in June when the baby comes.''

For a few minutes silence reigned. ''Before you go to sleep,'' I said, ''there are two other things I want to ask you. First, why is it that I find myself kipping down on this wretched sofa, when I seem to remember you were the noble one who volunteered to 'suffer the springs and narrows of this outrageous couch'?''

"That's easy. I've done it for your peace of mind really, for I knew you would be unhappy if a woman in my condition were subjected to any extra discomfort.''

"How very, very kind of you, thank you so much! The other thing is a bit more serious. To be honest, I've got the jitters. All the stuff in the Service about what I have to do, all that fighting talk about militant leadership. People do seem to be expecting a lot of me. I'm not sure I'm up to it, maybe old Peto was right. So you see, in spite of my brave answers in the Service, and my brave face afterwards, I'm scared. Does that make me a hypocrite?''

"No, it doesn't make you a hypocrite,'' she said, ''it makes you human. For goodness sake, try to stay that way. You didn't promise anything tonight as a solo effort: 'The Lord being my helper', wasn't that the phrase? Isn't the idea supposed to be that you are in partnership with God in this business? I think you should get it into your head that I am the only sleeping partner you've got — God is the other sort. Now how about letting your sleeping partner sleep!''

I closed my eyes and tried to follow suit but there was still enough adrenaline coursing through my veins to keep my mind active. I could hear again the vivid description from Dick Chaplin of the tactics used to deter the other aspirants for the job. It was only an hour or so since that conversation had taken place, and it had left a vivid impression, particularly with the closing sentences. He had finished with a half-humorous apology, almost a plea of mitigation. ''Don't think too badly of us, Vicar, for as you'll soon discover, we were not telling complete whoppers, just being a bit selective and emphatic, that's all. We didn't invent anything, just underlined a few things. Nothing wrong with that, is there?''

What could he mean? I wondered. I nestled my head once more into the pillow propped on the arm of the sofa and started to drift away. When I did fall asleep I dreamt of rats — they were all over the place; some of them as big as young cats. And the noise! It was like being in Hamelin at the time of the Pied Piper:

''With shrieking and squeaking
In fifty different sharps and flats.''

CHAPTER FOUR

All creatures great and small,
All things wise and wonderful,
The Lord God made them all.

(Mrs. C. F. Alexander, 1818-1895)

When the Vicarage rats did eventually make their entrance on the scene they did so in style, purloining a pound of Dairy Milk chocolates and sampling a dozen bottles of wine.

It was Mothering Sunday morning and the March sunshine gave promise of an early spring. After the eight o'clock Communion Service, I was breakfasting with the family in the kitchen. The warmer weather had allowed us to start sleeping upstairs but the splendid open fire in the kitchen still drew us to that room like a magnet.

Mark handed over his home-made Mothers' Day card. "Now close your eyes, mummy," he said, and taking my hand we moved together to the splendid oak-panelled dining-room. There was a large built-in cupboard there in which we had hidden a box of chocolates.

Then came dismay! The box was still there, though the top had been gnawed off; the individual wrappings were there too, but not one single solitary chocolate. I also kept the Communion wine in the same place and saw at a glance that the intruders had bitten their way into the cardboard container and chewed through every one of the twelve corks of the unopened bottles that were inside.

I had been in this cupboard only the evening before when everything had been perfectly normal, so it was obvious the visitors had worked very hard on a night shift.

Joyce was still pretending to have her eyes shut when we returned with the sad news. She soon opened them wide with horror as the message went home. I had already related the way would-be Vicars had been deterred from accepting the Benefice and she had been highly amused, but I had expurgated that part of the story that featured rats. Debt and rodents were the two great phobias in her life. Even now, I toned it down as much as I could by suggesting that mice were responsible.

"Oh my stars!" she exclaimed, "mice again. I thought we had left all that behind us in our last home. Promise me you'll get the pest-controller from the Town Hall tomorrow ... please."

I promised, not really needing any urging, for I suspected we were dealing not with mice, but their big brothers. To pacify her even further, I made a show of setting all four mousetraps we had bought in Chorley. Using bacon-rind as bait, I put two traps in the cupboard itself, and two in the cellar that lay immediately beneath that part of the house. It was good psychology I hoped, and I tried to underline the reassurance with, "We'll probably have caught them before the man from the Town Hall turns up tomorrow."

She gradually became more relaxed about it and by breakfast the next day was able to treat it with a bit of humour. "Whatever you do," she said, "please don't borrow any more cats, leave it to the expert. He has promised to come, hasn't he?"

I had phoned the Town Hall half-a-dozen times after getting in from Morning Prayer before finally getting through and obtaining the promise that the rodent operator would pay us a visit. I told Joyce, "This afternoon is the earliest he can make it, but don't worry, he will definitely be here today."

And he was as good as his word. He turned up just as I was setting out to make an emergency visit to the local hospital. I had actually got to the gate but went back and propped my bike against the house as his ramshackle car chugged into the drive. I stood there waiting to greet him as he slid across the front seat to the passenger side to get out.

"That door doesn't open," he said, nodding to the driver's side. We shook hands before he turned to the boot and extracted a large battered gladstone bag. "My equipment," he explained, patting the bag proudly. "In here," he said, "I have three different kinds of poison, the latest type of trap, and one or two devices of my own making. I am, what you might call, very well equipped for the task that lies ahead and come prepared mentally and physically to 'fight the good fight with all my might'."

I was not sure whether the monologue was specially tailored for a parson, or whether this was his usual style, but I quickly realised he was quite a character. His appearance intrigued me greatly.

He was a tiny man, maybe five foot tall, whose narrow face was blessed with a long pointed nose under which sprouted a dark bushy moustache. There was hair too on his face in the form of mutton-chop sideboards in front of prominent ears that came out at an unusually wide angle. The hair on his head was black and oily, brushed straight back with a parting dead centre. The black suit he wore was shiny with age, and a tie of the same colour went round a stiff wing-collar. His movements were quick and jerky as he stepped round me to get a better view of the house.

While he looked at it, I looked at him and the thought flashed through my mind that this was very odd indeed. I had heard it said that some people married to each other for a long time begin to resemble each other; the suggestion has even been made that some folk begin to look like their dogs; but here was a man who actually looked like his job or, at least, one aspect of it. I could think of various parts in pantomime or children's plays for which he would have needed very little make-up! A natural for Ratty in 'Wind in the Willows', for instance. For some reason my confidence in his abilities grew.

"I'm on my way to the hospital," I said, "but I would like to tell you why I have asked you to come." He listened intently

as I filled in the details of my experience the previous day. I concluded the account with an expression of surprise that the rats had eaten every single morsel of chocolate in the box. "Not even a crumb left," I explained.

"No, no, no," he said, with a smile that showed his small very white teeth, "they didn't eat them, they wouldn't do that. What they actually did was take them away to their nest." He continued by giving me a graphic description of how this was done. "Mother rat gets hold of a chocolate like this." He held up both arms to demonstrate. "She holds it tight against her chest and then lies down on the ground on her back. Father rat takes her tail between his teeth and pulls her back to the nest with the booty. I've known them move a dozen eggs that way without breaking a single one."

I was suitably impressed. "Let me take you first to the cellar where I suspect they live," I said, "then I must go to the hospital. When you want to go into the house, just walk in. I've left the back door open and my wife is expecting you. By the way, what's your name?"

"Jolly," he replied, "Amos Jolly; but most people just call me Mister Ratcatcher ... like they call you Vicar, I expect."

"OK Mr. Jolly, this is the way." I took him round the side of the house to the cellar door at the rear. I used my yale key and we entered the dark gloomy place which smelt of dampness. I reached out for the light switch but he grabbed my hand anticipating what I was about to do. With a gesture he indicated that he preferred his own type of illumination. The gladstone bag was opened and a long silver torch extracted.

"Sh ... sh ... sh," he whispered with a finger to his lips. And then to my surprise he dropped to his knees. I thought he was looking for droppings until I noticed that his head was up; his eyes appeared to be closed as he started sniffing; then on all fours he moved a yard forward and repeated the process.

After a few minutes he rose slowly and came to stand by

my side. With his mouth almost touching my ear, he whispered a question: "Do you keep ferrets?"

"Ferrets?" I repeated, in a whisper of surprise.

"Ferrets," he said again, "for rabbitting, you know."

I did not know actually so I shook my head thinking that it would be hard to imagine a more unlikely ferret-keeper and rabbitter than myself, as I stood there in my clerical greys and highly polished shoes. "Must go now," I whispered, "I'll leave you to it." He nodded and raised a hand in farewell, before dropping down again on hands and knees.

I was glad to get out into the open again and had walked a dozen yards in the direction of the back door when I was brought to a halt by a loud piercing cry that froze my blood. Startled, I stopped and turned towards the cellar from where the loud cries of anguish were coming. "Ouch, ouch, ouch," I heard as I hurried back. I had a vision of the good Mr. Jolly being attacked by a regiment of rats.

It suddenly dawned on me that maybe rats were not responsible for the uproar, and I stopped short of the door. A loud torrent of invective was flowing out like a river in full spate. I suddenly realised it must have been one of the mousetraps that had caused Mr. Jolly to lose his cool; no doubt his hand had triggered it off as he crawled forward on the flagged floor.

Working on the principle that discretion is the better part of valour, I retreated to avoid confrontation with a very irate ratcatcher, climbing the stone steps into the house. As I ascended, I could hear from below a choice selection of language the like of which I doubted had ever been heard in the Vicarage before. Not that it lacked a certain theological flavour, for I noticed there were frequent and colourful references to that place where souls unfit for heaven are said to dwell. On a more personal level, I was aware that both my intelligence and parentage were being seriously questioned.

Joyce was given a quick resume of events before I went out through the front door to the bike and the hospital. On my

69

return an hour later, I was given a blow-by-blow account of the succeeding events that had left her helpless with laughter.

"Hello, hello, anybody at home?" she had heard soon after my departure.

"Come in Mr. Ratcatcher," she had called out, using the form of address I had told her to employ. "I'm in here, first door on the left."

"Mr. Ratcatcher eh! I like it. Ratcatcher! First time I've been called that," said a deep bass voice as the kitchen door opened and the Diocesan Bishop walked in. Joyce's face must have been a picture.

"Hello, Mrs. Brown," he said, "I heard your little boy has been down with pneumonia and since I was in the area I thought I would call and see how he is. But Ratcatcher? Is that how you think of me? Mind, it's not a bad description of some aspects of my job." His hearty laugh echoed through the house.

There was a quick apology and a quick explanation. The genial Doctor Baddeley, who had been Bishop of Melanesia and then Whitby before Blackburn, drew up a chair by the fire and tickled Mark under his chin while Joyce went into the smaller kitchen to make a cup of tea. Then came another tap at the back door. This time it was the Bishop's turn. In his deep powerful voice he bellowed, "Come in Mr. Ratcatcher, come in!"

Mr. Jolly appeared through one door as Joyce came in from another bearing the tea tray. A grubby-looking handkerchief was tied round his right hand.

"Nearly lost my bl**dy fingers," he complained, holding up the damaged hand as evidence. Then seeing the clerical collar in front of him, he apologised for the language. "Blinkin' fingers, I should have said, sorry." Then to show he had good cause for his anger he added, "Vicar here must be a bloo.. a flippin' idiot. Some of 'em are damn fools, aren't they?" He looked for endorsement to the Bishop.

The Bishop grinned broadly. "Must admit it's not the first

70

time I've heard that charge." He quickly changed the subject from clergy to rats. "How have you gone on in your professional capacity? Any luck? What's the score?" he enquired.

The damaged fingers were forgotten as Mr. Jolly launched into a full description of his findings and activities. He became very animated as he expressed his confidence at the final outcome of his endeavours. "I'll get the little bu ... the little blighters, don't you worry," he said with a reassuring look in Joyce's direction. He accepted the invitation to a cup of tea and pulled up a chair to the other side of the fire.

"I'll show you where the cloakroom is," said Joyce, "for I expect you will want to wash your hands."

"No need for that," replied Mr. Jolly as he rubbed them vigorously on the front of his jacket and then, as though for extra hygiene, down the side of his trousers. "If I washed my hands after every little job I do, I would soon have no skin left on them." He leaned forward and took a piece of fruit cake from the plate Joyce was offering.

After a bite, he addressed the Bishop. "I expect you know that they say we all have to eat a peck o' dirt before we die: that's right isn't it?"

"Well, yes," admitted the Bishop with a twinkle in his eye, "but I don't think the peck has to be eaten at one sitting, as it were. Surely, it can be spread out over a fairly long period."

This evoked a grin from the ratcatcher. He took a greater interest now in this clergyman who had indulged in a spot of leg-pulling. "Which is your parish?" he asked.

"Haven't got one."

"Well, I hope you soon will."

"Thank you."

"Fellow here is a lot younger than you and he's managed it. And he's not exactly blessed with brains, is he, or he wouldn't go round leaving mousetraps all over the place."

"Quite so," agreed the Bishop with mock gravity.

For a quarter of an hour they sat there chatting, mainly about Mr. Jolly's engrossing occupation, until they both remembered they had other things to do.

They left together. The Bishop leaving his blessing; Mr. Jolly his solemn promise that he would not rest day or night until "the cunning little devils" had been completely annihilated.

Joyce waved them off and admitted later that she felt better for both their visits. His Lordship had left a rather enigmatic message for me. "Tell RB," he had said with a smile, "that I'm glad I found him out; and that in future I think he should remember the New Testament injunction to catch men doesn't mean in mousetraps."

The red Vauxhall flying the Diocesan pennant moved to the gate followed closely by the dilapidated Austin Seven. One turned left, the other right, onto the very busy A6 that passed within a few yards of the Vicarage gate.

Before the coming of the motorways this was one of the busiest roads in the country, a main north-to-south artery, and it ran right through the middle of my parish. It was not dubbed 'Murder Mile' for nothing and often I was involved in coping with the consequences of serious accidents. But the road had its joys too, for the speedy travel it allowed was particularly useful, for instance, when I rushed Joyce to hospital a few months after the Bishop's visit for the birth of our daughter, Janet. And it was June, and warm, and we were happy and comfortable.

The main road also brought us a constant stream of callers for it was a highway much used by tramps. Our large stone house, covered in part with ivy, was easily identified as the Vicarage by its proximity to the church and must have seemed an obvious oasis for refreshment and assistance.

We decided early on that we would never refuse food and drink but our financial straits ruled out the possibility of monetary assistance of any significance.

It was not unknown for some of these 'gentlemen of the

road' to complain about the fare we provided. In fact, we quickly discovered that there was no truth in the old adage that beggars can't be choosers! For instance, there was the bearded, doleful tramp who told me with emphasis that he would jolly well stop coming if I persisted in using margarine instead of butter. Another asked me how I had been brought up if I did not know better than to leave a sliver of fat on a beef sandwich, and yet another brought his mug of tea back to the door with the request that he would prefer Earl Grey if I did not mind. But by and large, the system worked reasonably well with the men enjoying the rest and refreshment the halt provided.

Joyce was painting the sitting-room ceiling one autumn day when a tramp came knocking on the window where she was. Hurrying down the step-ladder she went to the door. "Madam," he began, "I couldn't help seeing what you are doing and, quite honestly, I don't think that's a job for a woman."

Joyce looked him over. He was reasonably clean and tidy. "I'll make you a cup of tea," she said.

"That's not what I want," came the reply. "As a matter of fact, I am a trained painter and decorator, served mi time, I did, and I'll tell you what; make me a nice meal, give me half-a-crown, and Bob's your uncle! I'll finish the painting and make a smashing job of it too. Is it a deal?"

Joyce hesitated, for apart from the children she was alone in the house, but after a few more pleas and assurances she caved in. "OK," she finally said with some misgivings, "this way, and I'll show you what I'm trying to do."

"It's only the ceiling that's being painted," she explained when they were in the sitting-room, "for to be perfectly honest we can't really afford new wallpaper, so it's very important to avoid any splashes on the walls. The coal-fire in here tends to smoke when the wind is in the wrong direction and that makes the ceiling look dirty after a while. You can see how careful I've been so far to keep the paint off the walls; do you think you can do the same?"

He was affronted by the question. "Madam," he protested, "you don't know who you're talking to! Do you realise that I once papered and painted the Mayor's Parlour in Wigan Town Hall. You've no need to tell me how to tackle a fiddlin' little job like this." He took the brush and mounted the step-ladder as Joyce went into the kitchen to make egg and chips.

Having wounded his pride once, Joyce did not dare either wait and watch or return for an inspection until the meal was ready some twenty minutes later. Then she nearly collapsed in dismay when she saw the havoc he had created in such a short time. "Oh my stars!" she cried in disbelief as she surveyed the scene, "what a mess, what a terrible mess. I must have been mad to allow this to happen." There was more white paint on the walls, floor and tramp than the ceiling.

"Please come down at once," she commanded, almost weeping in anguish. "Come on, follow me to the kitchen for your meal, and then please go." She stood outside the cloakroom while he scrubbed some of the paint off hands and face. When he came out, rubbing his hands in anticipation of the food, he was no longer looking sheepish, but was now on the offensive. "You've a cheek, missus," he said, "fancy giving me a Woolworth's paint brush and expecting a good job; and anyway, those one or two spots on the wall will soon wash off. Can't think what you're going on about."

Soon he was sitting at the kitchen table eating noisily and greedily, wiping his mouth from time to time with the back of his hand. It was when he had got to the stage of cleaning the plate with chunks of bread that he brought up the subject of murder. As he popped the last wipe into his mouth, he pushed the plate away with a belch and said, "Isn't it strange that four women have been 'done in' round here this last year?" He positively leered at Joyce as she stood on the other side of the table. "Cut up in pieces they've been, blood all over the place. Bet they all got a shock when the knife went in." He laughed as though the recitation of such things gave him pleasure. With obvious relish for the tea and the subject he drained his cup with a loud "Ah ... ah ... ah," before continuing. "Must have been somebody who gets into their houses by false pretences and then finishes 'em off."

There was no mistaking the deliberate menace in his words and manner. "Just the kind of thing I could do, I mean getting into their homes as a tradesman, you understand, for women are always glad of a bit of cheap decorating." He picked up the table knife and tapped it several times on the empty plate. "Now then, let's settle up shall we? The deal we made was that you would feed me and give me a pound, that right?" The knife was still tapping the plate.

Joyce told me later that this was the turning-point. There was a struggle in her mind between fear and anger, but only for a moment. Her Geordie blood was up and she was determined to be neither cheated nor terrorised by this rogue.

On the sideboard behind her was a half-cut loaf and a large bread knife. She turned and picked up the knife. Holding it upright she took a pace to the table before banging the bone handle on the surface immediately in front of the tramp.

Her eyes were flashing with anger as she drew herself up to her full height of five-foot-three; all eight stones of her quivering with emotion, as she banged the knife on the table again and again. "What makes you think it was a man who committed the murders?" she shouted, "women can be violent too. In fact, where I come from in Durham there was a woman, Mary Ann Cotton, who's in the Guinness Book of Records with fourteen deaths to her credit. Have you got the message! Out now, out before I lose control of myself, out!" She flung a sixpenny piece on to the table. "Take that, your fare to Preston, and vamoose. You know jolly well you don't deserve even that after the mess you've made. Now S-C-R-A-M!"

The transformation from bully to abject cringing coward took less than three seconds. He was out of his chair in a trice, half running to the door, stopping only to collect his haversack which he had deposited in the sitting-room on his arrival. There were no goodbyes as he sped through the front door opened and held by Joyce. "Don't you dare ever to come here again, or you'll have me to deal with," was her parting shot.

She banged the door shut and bolted it, still shaking with passion, before flying up the stairs to make sure the children were all right. They had both had an afternoon sleep but now Mark was standing in his cot playing with the beads along the top, while Janet was just beginning to cry for food. She lifted them to her, cuddling them both, as she tried to calm herself and cool down.

Soon afterwards I arrived back after an afternoon spent traipsing the streets and knocking at doors. Joyce had calmed down considerably by this time and was able to relate the events of the afternoon with a broad grin on her face. She said, "Until he went through the door and down the drive, I had always believed that not being able to see someone's heels for dust was just a figure of speech!" I guessed that part of her high spirits came from her sense of relief that the episode had ended as it had.

"Come and look at the mess," she said as she led the way into the sitting-room. There was no escaping the fact that the walls would have to be repapered. I told her I had seen some cheap rolls of paper on the market and that we ought to be able to afford the £5 or £6 they would cost. "And although I've never done it before, I have always wanted to have a go at papering a room. Of course, I'll need a labourer, and I'll give you three guesses who it will be."

I turned to see her reaction but she was not listening. Instead she was looking carefully at the mantel-piece over the tiled fireplace. "Have you moved the brass carriage-clock?" she asked anxiously.

"Of course not, why would I do that?"

An angry flush spread on her face. "If I were not a Vicar's wife," she exclaimed, "I would now say a very big damn! In fact, I'm going to say it anyway: DAMN, DAMN, DAMN! I really treasured that clock. It was a family heirloom, over a hundred years old." She stamped her foot in frustration and anger.

"I'll bet there's one tramp in this area who will never dare to ring our door-bell again," I said, "and I wouldn't like to be in his shoes if he does — at least, not if that bread knife is within easy reach of you. I reckon you would make Mary Ann Cotton look like a Sunday School teacher. But you know, she was a poisoner, whereas you are obviously better with a knife!"

"Live and learn," said Joyce, "but it's been an expensive lesson and I shan't be so stupid again."

To make her feel a bit better I promised to scrub the paint off the floor while she was out at the Mothers' Union Meeting that evening. It was hard going and I was covered in sweat at the end of it but I was pleased with the result. That was true also of my first attempt at paper-hanging a few days later. Joyce offered to write to the Mayor of Wigan strongly recommending me for work in the Parlour there when the time for redecoration came. "And every cloud has a silver and gold lining," she said as she admired my handiwork and the bright new wallpaper.

It was soon after this that we made an interesting discovery about our stone gate-posts. Joyce and I went out to look at them more closely than ever before. In my hands was a copy of *The Sunday Times*. She got quite excited as she pointed to the several chalk marks clearly visible on the uprights. Her finger was moving on the open page of the newspaper as I held it for both of us to see. "I knew it," she said, "I knew it."

There was a feature article that day on the subject of the sign-language used by tramps to pass on information to those who shared their life-style. Pointing to an illustration of a small cross inside a circle she read, "This sign means that the occupants will provide a meal." She turned to the gate-post. "Look, there it is, exactly the same." She quickly found another hieroglyphic on the post that matched one in the newspaper. "This wriggly line on top of a square means that they will get you a bed at a nearby hostel."

"And look at this one," said an animated Joyce thrilled at the discoveries, "this one at the top means we will cough up a bus fare." The other post was also a mine of information indicating among other things that we posed no threat and on a 'push-over scale' of one-to-ten (illustrated by a line divided into segments) we were rated at eight-and-a-half. "Of all the flippin' cheek," I said, "we must need our heads reading."

But Joyce had disappeared, only to come into view again minutes later with a bucket and scrubbing-brush. Soon our gate-posts were the cleanest in the parish ... but not for long. After drying them with a cloth, she extracted from her skirt-pocket a piece of chalk, and with advice from me and *The*

Sunday Times proceeded to produce a most formidable set of messages for those skilled in the art of decipherment. Our gate-posts now indicated that we had a fierce dog, an uncharitable disposition, and an extremely close relationship with the local constabulary. We laughed our way indoors, pleased with our artistic endeavours.

And we had every reason so to be, for our efforts were rewarded with success, and in the days that followed our vagabond callers were few and far between. For a while the burden was lightened, yet we could console ourselves that the genuinely needy would still call. We had found a way of deterring the professional scroungers. But alas, we were soon back to normal, more or less, for the rain washed off our signals in due course, and the 'safe place' where I had placed the newspaper for future reference could neither be found nor remembered. We did from time to time wash the gate-posts but the splendid immunity we had enjoyed for a short time never returned.

It was not only tramps who felt they had the right to make demands on a clergyman, presuming that behind every clerical collar there lurked a Good Samaritan. Flattering and demanding, with the requests for help coming in many shapes and sizes, some of them odd and unexpected, like the time I picked up the telephone to be asked if I had yet received some cremated remains through the post. "Thought I'd better phone and tell you I'd sent them or you might have wondered what they were, for they are not in a casket. They'll be with you in the morning, I expect."

"Sorry, I'm not with you. What are you talking about?"

"Father's ashes. I've parcelled them up and sent them through the mail. We want them to be buried in the family grave and I didn't fancy carrying them with me from London. My sister in Preston will come with me for the interment; we'll buy a casket there. We shall be with you the day after tomorrow at two o'clock. Goodbye."

It was all rather peremptory with little opportunity to get

a word in edgeways. I awaited the arrival of the parcel with some apprehension. And with good reason as it turned out.

It left a faint trace of grey dust on the hall floor when I picked it up. The package was flat and remarkably light in weight. I suspected it had been leaking all the way from London. Inside the brown paper parcel was a cellophane bag with a slit in one of the seams. I was worried by the fact that there was a serious shortage of ashes for the casket the women would bring.

Wearing rubber gloves in the interests of hygiene and because of my distaste I transferred the ashes to a similar cellophane bag and again their paucity gave cause for concern. For a moment I was tempted to eke them out with talcum powder but a trial dash on the back of my hand from the tin in the bathroom indicated that it was a bad match. It occurred to me that the nearest thing to ashes is ashes and it was a short step then to the kitchen grate with its plentiful supply. Thankfully Joyce was out with the children when I perpetrated the deed, so I was able to use her baking-board and rolling-pin to reduce the pieces of cinder to the right consistency. The colour left something to be desired, but it was the best I could do and, erring on the generous side, I filled the bag and sealed it with sticky tape. It was then placed in the original container which had a purple cross printed on it.

I was completely satisfied in my own mind that this was a kinder thing to do than tell the daughters that their father's remains were wedged in a crevice in the floorboards of the guard's van of the Flying Scotsman, condemned for ever like the Wandering Jew to travel through the land until the Day of Judgement. It was with a clear conscience that I stood with Tom twenty-four hours later, clad in my clerical robes, awaiting the arrival of the two ladies for the simple service of burial. Tom was the seventy-year-old Sexton, a splendid, straight-speaking, native of the village, looking very dignified in his black Verger's gown, his snow-white hair moving gently in the breeze.

At the appointed time the taxi arrived at the church gate and out stepped an attractive woman in her early forties, tastefully dressed in a black suit, white blouse, and large picture hat. Black suede shoes with gloves to match and a pearl necklace completed the outfit. Her deportment matched her elegance as she advanced towards us. "Blimey," said Tom out of the side of his mouth, "a duchess, at least!"

"The Vicar, I presume," she said as we shook hands. Her voice had that brand of affectation known locally as "lah-di-dah". The description "posh" was reserved for the genuine article. She ignored Tom completely as she turned and waited for her much more ordinary tweed-clad sister to come alongside, carrying a highly polished oak casket.

Tom was holding the ashes on a brass offertory plate. We had been puzzled as to how best to hold and carry them. The 'duchess' took them up while her sister opened the casket lid; she held them almost tenderly between gloved hands for a few seconds before placing them gently in the box. I was doubly glad at that moment that I had made the package feel right.

Taking the casket from her sister the 'duchess' turned to Tom. "Carry this carefully," she said in imperious tones as she thrust it into his arms. "Now, my man, lead us to the grave." There were no "please-and-thank-yous", and I could see Tom's eyebrows twitching in irritation as we formed our little procession and began slowly to make our way past the main entrance of the church to the family plot behind the west wall.

We stopped at the place where Tom had dug the small square grave. He knelt by the side of it ready to place the casket in its place, when the 'duchess' raised an objection. "Wait!" she commanded, "are you sure this is the right place?" Without giving Tom time to reply, she spoke to her sister, not in any way attempting to lower her voice, "You know, Emma, I don't trust these manual workers an inch; if they can get things wrong they will."

I gasped at the rudeness of her remarks and was on the point of issuing a rebuke when Tom beat me to it. He had been pushed to the edge of his patience and he now went over the top. "Don't come the high and mighty with me, Lizzie Dawes," he said, his face red with anger, "you might have posh clothes now and speak as though you had a plum in your mouth, but I remember you when you had holes in your stockings and a snotty nose; you might have gone up in the world a bit since you lived on Waterhouse Green but that doesn't give you the right to be so damned rude. So cut it out, what are you trying to prove?"

There followed an embarrassing silence. Then Tom in a quieter voice spoke again: "I've known your family all my life and, believe me, this is the proper grave. You know, we don't just dig holes anywhere, we do check properly."

I thought it was time I tried to take the heat out of the situation. "Are you all ready for me to begin the Service? I've got a copy of it for you both here. You'll be able to follow it." I handed out the printed sheets.

Ten minutes later it was all over. I turned and shook hands with them both. There was no discomposure evident as the 'duchess' swung round to face Tom. With a smile she held out her hand, "It's Tom Bowker, isn't it?" she said, "forgive me, I honestly didn't recognise you, and I do apologise if I upset you." Tom's handshake and smile conveyed the right impression. She handed him an envelope. "This should cover the fees, and I think there'll be enough to buy you a drink as well."

We walked with them to the gate where the taxi was still waiting. Even the way she got into the vehicle and sat looking straight ahead had a bit of style about it. As it moved off, we were treated to a 'Queen Mother'-type wave of the hand in farewell.

"I heard she'd married a rich bloke down south," observed Tom as we walked back, "but there was no need for all that hoity-toity business — and she used to be such a nice lass.

82

She was probably a bit tense today and didn't quite know how to play it. Sorry I lost mi temper.''

We were approaching the vestry door. I could see a small figure pressed against a stone buttress by the side of it. I went to investigate. It was Janet clad in a navy-blue raincoat that went down to her ankles — obviously she was wearing Mark's; the sou'wester was her own as were the wellington boots that completed her outfit. A light rain was beginning to fall so she was suitably attired. Over her shoulder, held like a guardsman holds his rifle, was a toy seaside spade.

''What on earth are you doing here?'' I demanded.

Back came a whisper. ''Have the mornings gone?''

''The what?''

''The mornings — those ladies at the funeral. I'm waiting to fill in. Tom's going to give me threepence if I help him.''

Tom's face spread into a broad smile as he verified the deal. ''Go on, take her with you,'' I said, ''and make her earn her money.'' Then to Janet: ''It's not 'mornings', it's 'mourners'. And I know why you've got Mark's coat on — it's to make sure you keep your own nice and clean, isn't it?! Anyway, you've got half-an-hour and then I'm coming for you.''

I left them and went to collect my bike from the Vicarage next door. I was wheeling it to the gate when Tom reappeared. ''Vicar,'' he called, ''I'd like a word before you go.''

I stopped and waited while he came to me. ''Which do you want first,'' he asked, ''the good news or the bad?'' He answered his own question by holding up the envelope the 'duchess' had given him. ''She's been very generous,'' he said, ''she's doubled your fee and mine and made a donation of twenty quid to the church. Isn't that good!'' He paused and his face clouded. ''The bad news is...''

''Yes, let's have it. What's wrong?''

''Well, to be honest, we've just buried that casket in the wrong grave. I've had a quick look at the churchyard plan, and she was right. It should have been on the other side of that tall gravestone. What should I do... any ideas?''

"Oh no! I don't believe it, Tom; what a mess!" I made a quick decision. "Take it up and put it in the right place. And say nowt to anybody. It might be a long time, if ever, before they come to the grave again, and then they will probably go to the right one. Gosh, wouldn't she gloat if she knew she'd been right all along! Do that and forget about it ... I'm off now ... so long."

I headed for Marsh Lane, determined to use the thirty minutes I had available to the best advantage. Mr. Sutch had a small farm there and he had telephoned earlier with a request for a visit. I knew his house well, for I had been there many times in recent months during the last long illness of his wife. I had not seen him since the funeral a fortnight before. And I was not likely to forget that occasion in a hurry! I had half expected there to be muffled sounds of protest from inside the coffin, for at that very time we were doing something completely contrary to the dead woman's last solemn request. I had been there at the death-bed scene when with her last breath she had extracted a promise from her husband that she would be buried in the parish of Charnock Richard. It had been very moving as Mr. Sutch, kneeling on the floor by the side of the bed, had held her hand and, with tears in his eyes, had acceded to her request. "Aye lass, aye, anything thou wants, thou can 'ave." With his free hand he managed to get his handkerchief from a pocket and wipe his eyes.

Half-an-hour later she had passed away. I sat with him and other relatives having a cup of tea. I was astonished when he began to make arrangements for the funeral to take place in my parish. I remonstrated with him in the strongest possible way. "Legally you have the right of burial at Whittle because you live in the parish but, Mr. Sutch, you have just given your word to a dying woman — surely you can't break your promise now."

"Can and will," he responded. "As you say, Vicar, I've the legal right. That's what I want, just mi rights, nothing more,

84

nothing less."

"But why?" I asked in bewilderment.

"Mi first wife's buried at Charnock Richard. That's where I'm going to be laid to rest. I don't want to be on top of this one; as a matter of fact I would like her far enough away in your churchyard. Mi mind's made up."

And it was. There was no shaking him. I had officiated at the funeral at the special request of the other members of the family, but had felt distinctly unhappy. All these things came vividly to mind as I pedalled my way to my first meeting with him since. And now he had asked to see me. I wondered why. Maybe he was feeling guilty and in need of Confession and Absolution. Somehow I doubted it but I would soon find out.

I propped my bike on the side of the porch and used the iron knocker on the door. It was an old farmhouse but Mr. Sutch did not farm the land. Most of it was rented to a neighbour but the other part was used for his thriving business of breeding dogs. The place smelt of them, around and inside the house.

"Good of you to come, Vicar," greeted this funny-looking little man as he led me down the passage I knew so well. In the living-room, he stood by the side of a square scrubbed table that occupied the centre of the room. He was small, not more than five foot tall, with a bald head, and dressed as usual in a blue boiler-suit with the sleeves rolled up. He did not look much like the wealthy and successful business-man he was — known throughout the area as one of the most expert dog breeders in the north of England.

"Not take much of your time," he assured me, "for I know you're a busy man as I am. And, as they say, time's money, but I did want to say a very big 'thank you' for your kindness over the past six months. I'll always remember how you gave the wife Communion and said those lovely prayers. Wanted you to know how grateful I am."

I acknowledged this with a faint smile and a deprecating,

85

"Oh, that's OK. It's my job." I wondered what all this was leading up to.

"I want to show my gratitude by making a donation to the church. But there's one condition." He produced something from his trouser pocket. "The condition is that this gift hasn't to be told to anybody, you understand, it has to be h'anonymous." He slapped on to the table with a bang, a half-crown piece, and repeated, "h'anonymous!"

I thought at first he might be joking, but a look at his face told me otherwise. I picked up the coin. "Thanks very much," I said, "I'll see it's put to good use. And have no fears, I'll not go spreading it around."

He saw me to the door and waited while I got on my bike. I was riding away as a thought struck him. "Vicar, Vicar," he called after me, "if ever you want a puppy, I'll let you have one cheap ... remember, cheap."

Without looking back I raised a hand in farewell as I speeded home. On arrival, I found that Joyce had already collected Janet from her 'filling-in' activities in the churchyard. Mark was listening to his sister's proud account of how she had earned the threepenny-bit she was clutching in her hand. He had been home from school long enough to don one of my cut-down clerical collars, his favourite piece of neck-wear. He was meeting boast for boast by indicating that threepence was small fry to the Rector of Brindle — the personage he always claimed to be when decked in his dog-collar. The argument was cut short by a summons to the tea-table.

As we concluded the meal, the church bells began to ring. Once a week, the local campanologists had a practice night, often attempting a two or three hour peal. The bell-tower was not more than fifty yards away and at times the house seemed to shake with the noise. It took some getting used to, but by and large we had managed it, and the children were generally able to go to bed and sleep in spite of it. We had a particularly fine peal of bells, and ringers from a wide area liked to come and try their hand. With a peal of eight bells, I was told, it was possible to ring more than 40,000 changes, a feat that would take practically a whole day.

There was to come a time, not long distant, when the bells rang non-stop not for a whole day but for, at least, six hours. When people in the streets asked why they were going on so long, they were told, "It's because the Vicar is leaving the parish!"

Ambiguous but true. Vicars were always 'rung in' and 'rung out' and sadly our time in the parish was coming to an end. I had been advised by my ecclesiastical superiors and by friends that I ought to accept the offer that had been made to me of another parish in a neighbouring Diocese. That day the bells rang was the day we were finishing our packing. They started at noon and went on until six-thirty when my final Service in the church began. It was a bitterly cold Sunday in January, almost exactly five years to the day from when we had arrived. Our last night in the Vicarage was as cold as the first. In the early hours of the morning we found the children in bed with us seeking warmth and comfort.

By six o'clock we were up and dressed; at eight the removal van came for our things. The church clock was striking midday as we went through the gate for the last time. There was a quick stop at Tom and Maggie's for tea and biscuits. We got warm there for the first time in more than twelve hours; then came goodbyes and tears. Finally, we were on our way. On our way to Bolton, to St Thomas's, Halliwell, in the Diocese of Manchester.

It was important that we should get there before the removal van, for obvious reasons. Thankfully, we managed it. A splendid bouquet of flowers on the doorstep lifted our spirits as we walked into our new home. A card with the flowers bore the simple message, "WELCOME TO ST THOMAS'S — May you be very happy among us."

Joyce walked straight to the cooker and turned on a gas-tap. "I'm afraid it's only eggs and bacon for lunch," she said, "will it do?"

CHAPTER FIVE

"Love your neighbour, yet pull not down your
hedge." 				(George Herbert 1593-1632)

I had sometimes wondered what it would be like to look down
the wrong end of the barrel of a gun. Well, now I knew!

I had gone innocently enough into the senior department
of the Sunday School with the intention of having a word with
Joe Kay, the superintendent, who also ran the Youth Club.
Since it was after three o'clock, I thought the young people
themselves would have gone home. In fact, I had met lots
of children streaming out of the other departments. But I
knew the teachers often stayed behind to clear up and have
a chat.

Joe was still there, and so was his particular class, about
a dozen of them, teenage boys and girls. To my astonishment
they were all lined up against the wall with their hands held
high above their heads. Standing menacingly in front of them,
holding a rifle in the hip position, was Desmond Bishop,
known as one of the bad lads in the parish, a leading member
of the local junior mafia.

"Get 'em up!" he was saying as I entered, "come on, higher
still." Teacher and pupils obeyed, looking very subdued. "And
now there's going to be a collection," he continued, "not for
the missionary society this time, but for yours truly. Come
on, one at a time, empty your pockets, and we'll begin with
…"

He stopped mid sentence as he caught sight of me in the
doorway. Swinging round on his heels, he pointed the gun
in my direction.

"OK, OK, Vicar," he said in a drawl that was reminiscent
of James Cagney in one of his gangster roles, "OK,

over there to the wall with the other guys. If you don't wanna get hurt, just do as you're told. Get a move on, I ain't got all day.''

I needed a few seconds to try to assess what was going on. At first I thought it might be a joke, and that they were all larking about. But there were no smiles; in fact some of the youngsters looked positively scared. I stared hard at Desmond and noticed he was perspiring slightly. He was a good-looking young man, going on for seventeen, smartly dressed, well groomed, as always looking immaculate, with his highly polished shoes and well-manicured hands. That is what had struck me about him when I had seen him for the first time. On that occasion he had been sitting in the corner of a cell in the local police station.

We looked at each other with the rifle between us, and I thought that maybe he was remembering that occasion too. What I had done that night, or rather failed to do, still rankled with him. He was most certainly not a member of the Vicar's fan club!

I had, in fact, refused to bail him out. The police had telephoned with the request that I should go and see him, and I suspected they too would have been glad to see the back of him. I went, but dug my heels in and said, ''No.'' I knew the Vicar before me had got him out of gaol two or three times, and he expected the new Vicar to do exactly the same. My natural inclination would have been to sign the form and take him home, but it was his mother who had pleaded with me to take a different course.

She had been very insistent when I had called to see her on my way to the police station. A little plump woman she was, in her early fifties, tremendously house-proud, who asked visitors to wipe their feet thoroughly before she let them into her shining sitting-room. She did not appear all that upset at the thought of Desmond being held in custody, but nevertheless what she said did seem to make good sense.

''He's been caught stealing a car again — it's the umpteenth time. Trouble is, he gets away with it too easily. Thinks he can snap his fingers and walk out. You see he's never had to spend a night in a cell before, but it would do him the world of good, maybe bring him to his senses. So please, don't let him talk you into going bail for him.''

And so I shook my head and refused when Desmond appealed to my charity, my sense of duty, my pastoral responsibility, and everything else he could think of. He certainly had the gift of the gab. Having failed in his appeal to my better nature, he switched to another tack, trying a spot of bribery. ''I noticed the other day, Vicar, that your garden is in a bit of a mess; get me out of this place and I'll be round first thing in the morning to tidy it up. I promise you'll be proud of it when I've done my stuff there.''

Again I shook my head. I had heard about his work in the Vicarage garden from the last Vicar, how he had picked all the flowers and sold them in bunches down the next street. The last thing I wanted was Desmond's horticultural assistance!

Thus I left him to spend his first night locked up. I had promised to go to court the following day and speak for him in front of the Magistrates, but this did not assuage his disappointment and anger. As I left him, he taunted me with, ''Call yourself a Vicar, you're rubbish. Not a patch on the last one. He would help anybody.''

The next day I had played my part in securing his release, but in Desmond's opinion that did not compensate for what I had refused to do. He found it hard to forgive and was generally hostile in his attitude whenever he saw me.

The old animosity was still there as he pointed the rifle and told me to get a move on. ''Join the others,'' he ordered, emphasising the command with a sweep of the gun. I took a few steps forward as though I was finally complying, but in reality I was still playing for time. I was puzzled by the beads of perspiration on Desmond's forehead. I was puzzled also by the fact that he was shaking slightly. He was normally so calm and cool. Imperturbability was his trademark, even in a tight spot, and he had been in plenty of those. I had seen him in the dock at the Magistrate's Court defending himself without turning a hair. It was completely out of character for him to get so worked up.

I put two and two together and came to the conclusion that he was nervous because he was bluffing. I did not think the seriousness of what he was doing would bother him too much, but the fact that he was vulnerable would. He was scared somebody would call his bluff. That could only mean one thing: that the rifle was a fake. I dropped my eyes for a closer inspection. It looked very suspect. I had seen children playing Cowboys and Indians with more realistic weapons.

There was a look of alarm in Desmond's eyes as I walked towards him. A note of panic in his voice too as I got close. "Stop where you are, Vicar," he said as he backed a couple of paces.

Then I lunged forward and got both hands on the rifle. There was no particular decision to do this, just an instinctive grab at the thing. Surprise was on my side, and with a violent twist, I wrenched it out of his hands. I held it above my head, out of arms' reach, as I delivered a stern rebuke.

"You stupid boy," I cried, relieved that he had let go so easily, "you need a flipping good hiding, and I'll get your father to give you one. And I've a good mind to call in the police. I'm telling you, if anything like this ever ..."

Desmond wasn't listening any more. He was off like a greyhound out of the traps, dashing for the stairs and the exit beyond. I turned to the group by the wall. Their hands were lowered now as they moved forward, each reacting in a slightly different way. Joe had taken it very seriously. "Gosh, Vicar, thank goodness you came when you did, who knows what might have happened?"

Some of the boys took refuge in bravado. "I was just getting ready to pounce on him," said one with a swagger. "I knew he was bluffing all the time," said another.

A couple of the girls were in tears, another was shaking slightly. Yet another saw the funny side. "He wouldn't have got much off me, there's only a penny and an old coat-button in my purse," she giggled.

I wanted to play the whole thing down as much as possible for I did not want the more sensitive youngsters to be in any way disturbed by what had happened. Perhaps even more, I did not want wild exaggerated stories to circulate among the parents with possible damage to the Youth Club and the Sunday School. When Joe made a little speech of thanks, saying how very brave I had been, I was quick to disclaim any such thing.

"You're being modest," said one of the older boys, "I reckon you deserve the VC" There were cries of "Hear, hear!"

"Listen carefully," I replied, "what I did had nothing to do with courage. I grabbed the gun because I knew it was a dummy. Look you can tell." I held it up for closer inspection. "A real rifle would have a broader stock than this, and the barrel would be thicker and longer. And look at this, bits of plastic for the sights! I could see it better than any of you. So you see, not bravery but observation; as Sherlock Holmes would have said, it was 'elementary, my dear Watson'."

I underlined what I was wanting to get across. "You were in no danger, not from a thing like this." To demonstrate the accuracy of my observations, I put it to my shoulder in a firing position and pulled the trigger. There was a loud bang and a bullet embedded itself in the door jamb. "Good Lord," exclaimed Joe, "it's a proper one!"

Suddenly I felt as weak as a kitten and had to sit down at a desk. I was told afterwards that my face went ashen, which was not surprising, for I went into a mild state of shock as it came home to me that I had actually struggled to get possession of a loaded gun; even the safety-catch must have been in the 'off' position. I sat there thinking what a silly fool Desmond was, what a dangerous silly fool.

"It's a 'Two-Two', Sir," said one of the lads examining the rifle, "you can kill rabbits with one of these." I picked it up to take to the Vicarage, and with as much reassurance as I could muster, shooed everybody home. I was glad of a cup of tea and a couple of aspirins when I was eventually sitting by my own fireside retailing the story to Joyce.

She did not think it at all funny, despite my attempt to add a note of farce as I described Joe and the youngsters lined up like prisoners of war against the wall. "Do you realise," she said, "how easily somebody could have been seriously injured or even killed? You must go round and see Desmond's parents at once. And if I were you, I'd hand the rifle to the police."

I did not accept her advice on either count. I felt I had had enough conflict for the time being, and decided I would take on Mr. and Mrs. Bishop after Evensong. They were a difficult couple to pin down to a real assessment of a situation. I had tried before, only to find that their concern was very superficial. Anything for an easy life was their basic philosophy, and they shied away from any action that involved time and effort. Decent enough people in their own way, their spotlessly clean home and material possessions took first place in their lives to the detriment of the children. Desmond, the youngest of three, was given a clean shirt every day, but not much love.

It was after Evensong that I called, accompanied by Walter Ashworth, one of the Churchwardens, a bachelor who lived alone. He knew the family well and, in fact having been born and brought up in the parish, there were very few inhabitants not in the same category as far as his knowledge of them was concerned. What is more, he was universally liked and trusted by all and sundry, for he had the rare gift of making every person he had dealings with feel important and valued. In a remarkable way, he enveloped a person he was with in his total interest. And it was not some kind of technique he had developed, but a genuine concern and respect for their value and integrity. He was just 'Walter' to young and old, rich and poor, church folk and non-church folk everybody. A truly exceptional man. I was glad of his company as we came to the house.

Apparently, Desmond's parents were out. I knocked and knocked but nobody answered. Finally, the next-door neighbour put her head round the door to say she thought they were away for a few days staying with friends in Blackpool. Walter and I walked to the Vicarage for a cup of tea. The route took us through the familiar streets of back-to-back houses, with not a 'semi' in sight; not a 'semi', in fact, in the whole parish of 5,000 people, and the only detached house was the Vicarage; the only trees, those few poor things in its garden.

A feature of nearly all the houses was that there was but one short step from living-room to street, a closeness to the outside world and to neighbours that I came to believe brought a special quality to the exceptionally warm community spirit which existed in the place. The houses were well kept and homely, but the simple architecture seemed to provide a backdrop that emphasised the fragility of life and the need for inter-dependence. It was but a thin front door that kept out the noise and dangers of the street; a thin front door that opened so easily to let in a friend.

It was a far cry from the drab streets of my Lancashire parish to the gates of heaven, yet that is precisely the route my thoughts sometimes took. It all stemmed from the phrase in the Apostles' Creed that I said daily — ''I believe in ... The Communion of Saints''. In this context, ''Saints'' are not those who wear haloes and live perfect lives, but ordinary folk trying with varying degrees of success to apply the principles of Christ to their lives. Their ''Communion'' is the supportive friendship they have with each other as a consequence.

To say ''I believed'' in this meant I appreciated its rightness and its value as an enrichment of human life. The frailty and inter-dependence illustrated in bricks and mortar, helped to create and maintain the fellowship I saw and admired. And the very same things had the power to turn eyes upwards as well as outwards, as from their frailty the folk looked for reassurance to the world of the spirit, needing to sense a reassuring fellowship with "that great cloud of witnesses" which the Bible says is there to provide encouragement to those running with patience the race that is set before them. I could not think it was a mere coincidence that as well as the special fellowship, there was in this same place too a noticeable reverence and expectancy in the public worship which I have rarely experienced elsewhere; a natural praying and praising with "angels and archangels and all the company of heaven".

This is not to say that such thoughts as these were uppermost in my mind as I made my way through these same streets several times in the days that followed the Sunday School disturbance, trying to make contact with Desmond's parents, but to no avail. The rifle lay hidden under the cushions of the settee in the lounge at the Vicarage. I was taking no chances, for I knew the lad was quite capable of a spot of burglary to re-possess it.

Then out of the blue one night his father turned up and requested its return. He produced a fire-arms' certificate. He sat in the study in rapt attention as I described the "hold-up" in full detail, his face expressing concern. Then came the expected wriggle. "I take this very seriously, Vicar, Desmond really is a very naughty young man. Quite honestly, I could break his neck! And the cheek of it, taking my gun for such a purpose. I'm grateful you haven't involved the police, he's been in enough bother with them already."

Then followed a series of threats against his son, ranging from stopping his pocket money, to "keeping him in" for a month. I had not much faith in either the implementation or the effectiveness of these measures. However, I had little option but to hand over the rifle, which I did with dire warnings of what I would do if his son was ever seen with it again.

"Thank you, thank you, Vicar, leave it to me," he said on his way out, "but I know you're a fair-minded man, and I'm sure you are willing to concede that Desmond is a bit of a joker, and in my own mind I think that's what it was all about — you know, a bit of fun, wanting to make people laugh." I closed the door in despair, leaned against it, and groaned aloud.

It was not a bit of fun either a month later when Desmond struck again. Rumour had it that he had lost a considerable amount of 'face' by the abortive robbery, for as word had gone round, he had come in for a fair amount of ridicule from his mates. I suspected it was an attempt to counteract this that led to his unprovoked attack on the Youth Club which met in the School on Sunday evenings after church.

I normally called in for half-an-hour on my way home. Desmond and two of his henchmen had minutes before wreaked havoc on the place, and I walked in as the dust was beginning to settle, with people still literally picking themselves up from the floor.

The record-player had been smashed to pieces and the records themselves thrown all over the place; the refreshment table had been up-ended, and broken glasses and cups were strewn around it; the song-books had been used as confetti, and torn-out pages littered the floor. Worst of all was the condition of Joe Kay, the Leader, who was sitting in a corner obviously very shaken, with his broken glasses in one hand and his handkerchief held up to an eye that was rapidly going black, in the other. Even though he was still dazed, he was by now trying to smile and pull himself together. He told me how he had tried to stop the hooligans as they had rushed in with their evil intent. He was so relieved that none of his youngsters had actually been hurt, even though three or four of them had been rough-handled and thrown down in the tornado-like raid.

There were many helping hands to clear up the mess. Joe was still holding the cloth to his damaged eye as he started to organise the evening's activities and get things as near to normal as possible. He was in his fifties, but always young at heart, devoting an enormous amount of time and effort to the youngsters in the parish. Even his annual holiday was spent taking them off to the Lake District each year, where he worked like a Trojan ensuring they all had a good time. Again and again he discovered there were more kicks than ha'pennies in what he was trying to do, but he exemplified one of the most important qualities a church worker can have, namely, 'stickability'.

It was through Joe, and people like him, that I came to see that perseverance is a very high form of love, and I was then able to endorse F. W. Faber's order of priority in his lovely Communion hymn: at one time I thought he had got it wrong, but then no longer.

> Multiply our graces,
> Chiefly love and fear,
> And, dear Lord, the chiefest,
> Grace to persevere.

The police were informed regarding Desmond's latest escapade but could do little about it for the simple fact was that he had disappeared. Soon afterwards his parents went to live near their friends in Blackpool and I lost touch with them. I found it was practically impossible to get any information about Desmond himself, and as the months went by I suspected he might be a 'guest' of Her Majesty somewhere! I had about two years to wait before I laid eyes on him again. Then, like the proverbial 'bad penny', he turned up one night at my Friday 'surgery'.

I had inherited and continued this system that was of value to the Vicar as well as parishioners. It was known and publicized that on a Friday evening the Vicar was 'at home' and available. Anybody could see him about anything from seven o'clock when he got in from Evensong until bed-time. It saved people from fruitless calls, and minimised the fag of answering the Vicarage door-bell. Generally, people came to arrange weddings or baptisms, or used the opportunity to talk over their personal problems and difficulties. The number of callers could range from two or three to twenty or more. It was not unknown for there to be people sitting all over the house waiting their turn to see me in the study.

Experience taught me how necessary it was to make a careful check on all the rooms in the house at the end of these sessions. This stemmed from an occasion when I thought I had closed the door on the last of my 'customers'. It had been a particularly busy evening and I was glad to flop into a chair in the dining-room (which we used as a sitting-room too) and start to unwind by watching a late film on television. We had supper on our knees, and eventually around midnight decided it was time to call it a day. After Joyce had gone up the stairs, I went round putting off lights and fires before following suit. Purely by chance, I opened the drawing-room door in case the light had been left on. It had not, but in the semi-darkness I made out an unfamiliar shape in the middle of the settee. Automatically I pressed the light-switch and then quickly wished I had not for I was sorry to embarrass the young couple sitting there, locked in a deep embrace.

They separated and blinked in the glare of the light. She got off his knee while he took out a handkerchief and started to wipe some of the lipstick off his face which he must have sensed was there. He straightened his tie, she smoothed her dress, as they stood up rather awkwardly giving me a faint smile.

"What on earth are you doing here at this time?" I asked not very intelligently, as I tried to keep a straight face.

"I came to ask you to sign my application for a passport," said the man. "Mrs. Brown asked us to wait in here."

The girl chipped in next. "We thought you were a long

time, but we didn't like disturbing you. We could hear the television. But we didn't mind waiting, and we have been ... er ... quite comfortable."

That immediately got my vote as the understatement of the year! They followed me into the study for the long-delayed business of the passport application. The form and photographs were soon signed.

"Now what about yours?" I asked, turning to the girl.

She handed me a sheet of paper which she had produced from her leather shoulder-bag. Rather sheepishly she said, "My sister asked me to give you this."

"But this isn't a passport application — it's a Baptism form."

"That's right. It's for a week on Sunday. I promised my sister I'd let you have it tonight. I knew I'd be passing the Vicarage on my way into town to the pictures."

"Oh, I see," I said, beginning to see only too clearly. "So you didn't actually come here together tonight?" I could hardly believe what I was hearing.

The man took up the cudgels for his friend. "Well no, not exactly; in fact, we didn't. We met on the doorstep. Quite a coincidence really, for we used to go out together when we were at school. It's been great to meet her again after all this time."

After a minute's pause, and a conscious effort, I managed to lower my eyebrows, wipe away the incredulous smile, and with as grave a manner as possible escort them to the front door where I shook their hand and wished them goodnight.

Joyce thought it absolutely hilarious, as I expected, when I recounted the details soon afterwards. She sat up in bed, a broad grin on her face: "You could make a fortune," she teased, "put it on the Notice Board and in the Parish Magazine. How about 'Friday Night is Music Night on the BBC; but at the Vicarage, Friday Night is Wedding-Music Night and if you can't find a partner, we'll do it for you. Comfortable snogging accommodation for compatability-

100

testing provided free of charge'."

"How am I going to make a fortune if it's free of charge?" I countered.

"Don't be so slow on the uptake," she retorted, "what about the extra wedding fees, and surely you would feel justified in adding a ten per cent surcharge when you tie the final knot for those who first started to get entwined on our settee. Mind, you would have to watch it with the police, of course, for running an unruly house is still frowned upon in legal circles if not in ecclesiastical! And on that happy note I'll say, Goodnight." From that time on, I carefully checked the rooms each week.

It was a Friday night again, about a year later, when the same couple turned up once more — this time to arrange their wedding. It was smiles all round, and since there was nobody waiting, I was able to deal with them as soon as they arrived. It was as they were leaving that the girl with an impish smile expressed their thanks 'for everything', concluding with, "And I'm so glad you were much busier the first time we came!" They had indicated on the application form the hymns they wanted at the ceremony. I immediately recognised two of them from the numbers: it was the other that puzzled me — number 181. I turned it up in the hymn book and saw they had chosen 'God moves in a mysterious way, His wonders to perform'. Not a bad choice, I decided, in the circumstances!

The choice of hymns at weddings normally presented few problems. Most couples went for the suitable and popular ones from the repertoire of about twenty or thirty well-known hymns traditionally associated with the marriage service. Occasionally there would be an odd request, either because the bride remembered it from schooldays or because it was "grandad's favourite", or for some other special reason. After a rare spate of somewhat unsuitable selections, I had the irreverent thought that it would be highly illuminating to print a short commentary on the service sheet explaining the reason for the choice. I had in mind something like the following:

"As the bridegroom looks at his rich and indulgent parents, we sing:"

O God! Our help in ages past,
Our hope for years to come,
Our shelter from the stormy blast,
And our eternal home.

"As the bridegroom surveys his future in-laws sitting across the church, we sing:"

Christian, dost thou see them
On the holy ground,
How the troops of Midian
Prowl and prowl around?

"As the lovely bride arrives to take on for life this lazy ne'er-do-well, we sing:"

Who would true valour see,
Let him come hither!

A final hymn in this category would have needed no explanatory note. The words themselves say it all:

Fight the good fight
With all thy might.

However, such vain imaginings were kept well in control! And it was nearly always possible to comply with the wishes of bride and groom in this respect. Apart from vetoing 'Roll Out The Barrel' at the end of a publican's marriage; and 'Where will the baby's dimple be, on its face or on its knee', when the bride was obviously 'great with child', there were few disagreements. Like every other priest, I was aware of the privilege of sharing these happy and splendid occasions with those who came, however tentatively, for God's Blessing on their new life together. It is not that the Church 'controls' God, or can give Him to some and not to others, but rather that it can in a special and powerful way remind people of His presence and love. St Augustine's words often came to mind: "The whole of your task, brethren, in this life, consists in healing the heart's eye, through which God is seen."

Apparently, I was not in such a good and holy frame of mind that Friday evening when Desmond Bishop turned up to arrange his wedding. He was accompanied by a very pretty girl of about his own age. Rather fragile looking with a porcelain complexion and delicate colouring, she appeared meek and mild, quite demure in both dress and manner. His introduction consisted of a nod in her direction plus the one word, "Hazel". We got off to a forthright start. "She's pregnant, so we want to get married. As soon as possible, but I want the Curate to take the Service, not you." (I immediately surmised he was thinking again of his night in the police cell.) "Oh, and by the way, I've applied for a stall on the market, and I've given your name as a referee, OK?"

"You've got a nerve," I said in irritation, "don't you think you're a bit hard-faced coming here with such cheek and such demands. After all you've done around this place, I really ought to kick you out! And what do you honestly expect me to say to the market manager when he writes ... that you're a nice, reliable, honest chap? I'm jolly well not going to perjure myself for you."

He stood up immediately. "Come on," he snapped at the girl, "let's go!"

"Sit down, and don't be such a fool." The surprise must have registered on my face, for I was not the speaker. It came from the 'meek and mild' one who spoke with authority without raising her voice.

Desmond stood dithering, not knowing quite what to do. "Sit, sit, sit," said the same voice, as though bringing a disobedient dog to heel. He slithered back into his chair with the lugubrious look of a mastered spaniel.

She took over the interview, but in a self-assured and charming way. "Vicar, I do most sincerely apologise. When Desmond is nervous he gets very aggressive and rude. But can we please arrange for our wedding, and you must decide who conducts it, of course."

I got out the application form as well as the parish diary. The formalities were soon completed. "I'll ask the curate to officiate," I promised, "but I'll be there too for the prayers." Desmond sat there trying to smile as though in full control.

"And then there is this matter of the market stall," she said. "My father already has a business there, and he's prepared to set us up with a stall selling pots and pans and kitchen ware. For the last year, Des has been working for dad, and he's very good at it. If you could help by letting us use your name, I'll guarantee that we don't let you down. If you like, you could speak to dad and some of the other traders who know us there, before you commit yourself. It's just that we have to have a vicar or a doctor, or somebody like that, and we don't know anybody else."

"Leave it with me," I promised, "I'll do what I can to help." They got up to go. Desmond attempted a mild apology but failed. I shook hands. "Take care of that girl of yours," I said, "I think she could be the making of you."

In due course came the wedding and a few months later the Baptism. I suspected this had been her method of persuading her father to allow the marriage, as well as to set them up with the stall. In no time at all it seemed I conducted a second Baptism, and then a third. And the stalls multiplied at the same rate as the babies. Walking through the market one day I saw they had three. 'D Bishop & Sons' it said over the top. Trade seemed to be booming. Desmond left a group of customers to run after me. "Vicar, Vicar," he called as he chased along, and then when I stopped he handed me a five pound note. "This is 'con' money," he said, "I thought you ought to have it."

"'Con' money," I repeated, "you mean from conning people ... is that what it is ... well surely you don't expect me to accept it?"

"No," he replied, "'Con' money — 'conscience' money — for that time years ago when I damaged the record player — you know."

I accepted it with thanks as a donation to Joe and the Youth Club.

"There's just one other thing," Desmond said, anxiously looking over his shoulder at the stall, "you know we live at the back of the school playground. Those kids on a Sunday night don't half make a racket when they are on their way home. Can you please do something about it? Wakes up my children sometimes. Must admit, once or twice, I've felt like going out and duffing them up! Have a word with Joe, OK?"

"Sure," I replied, "I'll do that. But I wouldn't like to be in your shoes if Hazel hears about you threatening to duff up some of our youngsters."

He winced visibly as he rushed back to deal with a group of customers all wanting to take advantage of his special offer on frying-pans. I knew Joe would be glad to receive both the fiver and the complaint!

There was never a shortage of requests, complaints and problems in this as in any other parish, though quite often they had nothing to do with the life of the church as such. I felt we provided a very necessary 'safety-valve' for people to let off steam at times. Some of the callers at the Vicarage fell into this category. Knocks at the door were not confined to Friday evenings, of course, and an increasing number of people came not to see the Vicar but the Vicar's wife. Now that Mark and Janet were at school, Joyce was able to put herself and her nursing experience at the disposal of parishioners — the kettle was rarely off the boil as people sought out her sympathetic ear.

It was a medical problem with a difference that brought Mrs. Jackson to the Vicarage one Monday morning just after eleven. And it was me she wanted to see, not Joyce, which was a pity, for she arrived at a time when I was not just busy, but in a frenetic state of activity as I tried desperately in a race against time to get the Parish Magazine ready for the press before the deadline expired at noon. If I failed to meet it, the Magazine would not be ready for the weekend, causing all kinds of irritations and problems. It was a 'touch and go' situation as I pounded away with my two fingers at the typewriter; one of those months when very little 'copy' had been handed in, so I had plenty of space and empty pages to fill.

I had vaguely heard the door-bell, but the first I knew I was in deep trouble was when, after a tap at the door, Joyce's smiling face appeared with the announcement that Mrs Jackson was there to see me on urgent business. The door immediately opened more fully, and in walked the lady herself.

Of all the people in the world I did not want to see at that moment Mrs. Jackson would undoubtedly have topped the list. The parish gossip *par excellence*, she talked in an unending stream, with not so much as a comma, let alone a full-stop, to allow a word in edgeways, which is particularly frustrating when the word one has in mind is "goodbye". It was rumoured in the parish that she had learned to breathe through her ears!

She came in talking, the sentence having been started in the hall; something about she knew that Vicar Brown would be only too pleased to help. This large round woman in her late sixties, complete as always with a shopping basket on her arm, was still muttering as she lowered herself with a sigh of satisfaction into an easy chair in front of my desk.

"Good morning, Mrs. Jackson," I said loudly so as to superimpose my first sentence onto one of hers, "but I am very busy this morning, so please be as brief as you can. What

106

can I do for you?"

For once she kept it short. "It's mi teeth, Vicar," she said, tapping the front of the upper-set with her forefinger to emphasise the point. "Mi teeth." She now used both hands to lift her upper lip, exposing the teeth in all their fulness.

"What's wrong with them?" I asked, "they look all right to me."

"They don't fit ... don't fit, and it's no good pretending they do. I've had new teeth before but they've never been like this set. Before, I've sometimes had to file them down a bit with a matchbox, but this plate would need a Black and Decker to make it right. You don't think the dentist could have given me somebody else's set, do you?"

I told her I thought this highly unlikely.

"Well, Vicar, I hope you'll do something about it. The dentist has argued with me till he's blue in the face, insisting that they're perfect. Not 'im as 'as to wear 'em, is it?"

"Look, I'll tell you what. Later today I'll give him a ring, and ask him to see you again. I'll tell him about your visit, and explain how worried you are. I'm sure he'll give you another appointment. Then I'll come round and tell you when you have to be at his surgery. Is that OK?"

She was obviously very pleased, and her face broke into a broad smile as I came round the desk to her chair. I lifted the basket, and invited her to stand up and take it. When this succeeded, I started to coax her towards the study door, trying all the time to fill the silence with talk so that she could not get started. "Yes, I'll give him a ring, and he'll be able to make an adjustment... it's probably very little that's wrong with them, though it feels a great deal to you ... and they do look very nice teeth, sure you'll like them in time ..."

I turned the handle of the door, hardly able to believe I had been so clever. I was just about to shake her hand and ask if she would mind seeing herself out when, alas, Joyce walked through the open door with two cups of tea in her hand. "I'll bet you are both ready for this," she said.

107

It flashed through my mind that this kind of behaviour fully justified Queen Elizabeth I's strongly held view that the clergy should not be allowed to marry! I tried to convey this historical reflection in a hostile glare directed at Joyce. She got the message, but there was no suggestion of apology, only defiance, in the big false smile she turned on and off as her face disappeared round the door.

Even the temperature of the tea was against me, scalding hot, so I had to risk damage to mouth and throat as I tried to empty the cup at a record rate. Mrs. Jackson was interested in no such endeavour, but had launched herself into an account of her second husband's dental history. It was said locally that she had talked both of them to death, but I was not quite sure how this could be done from a medical point of view, so I reserved judgement. But as she went on and on and on, two possible causes of death came to mind. Suicide was an obvious one that had not occurred to me before, and the other was something that she was already beginning to inflict on me — hypertension! The fingers of both hands, between sips, were relentlessly drumming the desk-top. The minute-hand of my watch had somehow picked up the tempo of the fingers and was simply shooting round the dial at a ridiculous rate. It was now eleven-thirty.

Another five minutes were to elapse before I felt able to pounce. Then, talking at twice the normal volume in a simultaneous conversation, I was able to walk towards her once more, repeat the ploy of the shopping basket, get her to her feet, and edge her sentence by sentence to the door. Her first husband's feet were majoring in the monologue at this stage, but by the time we were at the front door she was actually listening to my reiteration of the promise that I would get her another appointment with the dentist.

"Thank you, Vicar, I'll wait now to hear from you. Hope it's not long. Want them right for Sunday. I couldn't join in the hymn-singing with them like this. That would never do. I love the hymns."

That stopped me in my tracks. Anxious as I was to bid her farewell, I could not let that pass without comment.

"The hymns, Mrs. Jackson?" I queried, "forgive me, but I don't understand. I've never seen you in church here during my time as Vicar. When do you sing hymns?"

"Oh, I don't go to your church, Mr. Brown," she said with a beaming smile, "I go to the Salvation Army every Sunday. To tell you the truth, I would have gone to see the Major this morning about mi teeth, but you know, he's such a busy man."

I closed the door behind her and literally collapsed on the floor in laughter. The commotion caused Joyce to reappear. "Haven't you anything better to do than that?" she asked, "I thought you had the Magazine to write."

"I'm going to do some deep-breathing exercises now," I said as I got up. "And then you can bring me another cup of tea. I've decided to relax and take my time. Might as well be hanged for a sheep as a lamb."

Later that day, with the threats and admonitions of the printer behind me, I went to Mrs Jackson's house with the details of her dental appointment. These were written on a postcard, for obvious reasons, and I bent low under her window to get to her door without being seen. Then, holding the spring-loaded letterplate with the fingers of my right hand, I pushed through the card before ever-so-slowly releasing the plate. Silently I glided away round the corner to safety. Mrs. Jackson had had enough of my time for one day, and I urgently needed to see Florrie and Maggie Clarke who lived nearby.

They were spinster sisters in their mid-seventies, with only a year or so between them. Alike in looks and manner, they lived in the house in which they had been born. I got the impression it had changed little during that time. It had got shabbier, of course, but they did not seem to notice, and although a bit threadbare and poverty-stricken, it was well-scrubbed and spotlessly clean, though the brown paint and faded wallpaper did not exactly make it the brightest home in the parish.

A square of coconut matting covered most of the floor, laid on top of wood-block-patterned lino, eighteen inches of which could be seen round the edges. A cloth pegged rug was spread in front of the iron and brass fender. At one side of the fireplace was an old rocking-chair for Maggie, and at the other side for Florrie a wooden armchair, with an adjustable stick in the back determining the angle of the upright support. I never saw the sisters change places.

The most important piece of furniture was the square table in the middle of the room, adorned with a plum-coloured plush tablecloth decorated with tassels at the corners. Two simple wooden chairs were pushed under the table opposite each other, while the other two in the set were placed one on each side of the mirrored dresser that stood on the wall across from the fire. In a corner, by the inner door that led to a small kitchen, was a treadle sewing-machine. Placed on top of the wooden cover was a large red plant-pot containing an aspidistra.

'Bless This House' pleaded an embroidered sampler over the mantelpiece, under which stood two brass candlesticks, one on each side of the clock. This was their pride and joy, and they recounted to me several times how with their father and mother they had economised and saved in order to get it. It was a cheap imitation of a traditional marble clock, with the wood painted black to resemble the real thing, and with its colonnades and classical style it carried off the deception reasonably well. There was nothing inferior about the loud strike with which it signalled the hour. A little 'ping' was all that was given to the half-hour, the 'silver chime', which gave its name to the whole clock.

Florrie's recent illness had changed the arrangement of the furniture slightly in recent weeks. She was lying in a bed placed under the window, with the rocking chair now alongside the wooden armchair on the other side of the fireplace. Maggie was rocking in it gently as I entered. As

I glanced at Florrie, I was saddened to see how quickly now she was deteriorating. Both were thin, frail, even bird-like, but I could see here the unmistakable approach of death. Her eyes were closed, her shallow breathing came from an open mouth. She wore a well-darned cardigan over her nightdress.

"I think she's worsening rapidly," whispered Maggie, "she hasn't had anything to eat or drink for two days. Normally she loves a cup of tea. I'm very worried about her. Here, Vicar, sit here." She pulled one of the upright chairs from under the table and placed it alongside the bed.

I took Florrie's hand and held it for a while. She opened her eyes and I was not sure whether she recognised me or not. "I'm going to say a prayer for you, Florrie," I said, "is that what you would like?" There was no response, but as I started the Lord's Prayer, her lips began to mouth the words, so I knew she was with us in spirit. There followed the special priestly ministry of Absolution and Blessing. Then, I turned to Maggie with a one-word question: "Coal?"

"Please," she responded. I went into the yard and filled a bucket. Carrying it into the house was getting a problem for her. Having a supply by the hearth was so much better than going for it a shovelful at a time. She told me there was nothing else I could do. "But I do hope Mrs. Brown will be round again today," she said as I made my farewell.

I carried away some of the sadness of the atmosphere, wondering how Maggie would cope with bereavement and loneliness. However, the gloom had to be jettisoned at the end of the street when I called into another home to admire the new baby and arrange the Baptism. There is an old Lancashire saying that when there is a funeral in one street, there's a wedding in the next. The parish priest has to learn to hop from one to the other without too much fuss. He has no shortage of opportunity to comply with St Paul's guidelines for Christian ministry: "Rejoice with them that do rejoice, and weep with them that weep."

A couple of hours later, with half a dozen more visits

completed, I was back in the Vicarage ready for a rest. I put the kettle on the gas-stove. The sound of Children's Hour on TV coming from the dining-room told me Mark and Janet were home from school. Joyce rushed in as I was filling the teapot, she was slightly flushed and breathless.

"Florrie Clarke has just died," she said, "about half-an-hour ago. Fortunately, the Doctor called on a routine visit soon afterwards, so we've got the death certificate. I've promised Maggie you'll go there again for the committal prayers. While you're away, I'll get tea ready. When you come back I'll go and lay her out. Is that all right with you?"

"Sure, but a cup of tea for each of us first — and for goodness sake, stop rushing about."

Later that evening, when the children were in bed, Joyce described an incident both macabre yet slightly comic. Even in the telling she laughed but was close to tears at the same time. It had occurred towards the end of the laying-out process, when Joyce was finally buttoning the nightdress that had become Florrie's shroud.

"I'm sorry, Mrs. Brown," interrupted Maggie, "but I have to ask you to do something special for me. I see that you have left Florrie's vest on. It's a good one and I could do with it myself. Would you mind please taking it off? I've got an older one if you want to put it on her but maybe she doesn't need a vest at all. I'm shamed at having to ask you to do this but I am a bit hard-up just at present, and it will save me having to buy one."

"So I did it, of course," said Joyce, "but it makes you realise how poor they have been. And yet they've always been such good givers, haven't they?"

"Yes," I agreed, "incredibly generous, both of them." Since I was the only person in the parish who could identify the numbers on the weekly Giving Envelopes, I was the only one who realised how sacrificial their contribution had been. I used to notice, for instance, that a rise in the Old Age Pension always resulted in an increase in their gift. It was obvious they calculated exactly the maximum amount they could offer.

"It's a question of commitment, really," I said, "I once heard a preacher say that you can give without loving, but you cannot love without giving. I have noticed that some of the key passages in the New Testament link giving and loving very closely, like 'God so loved the world that He gave His only begotten Son'; or 'Christ loved the Church, and gave Himself for it'; or again 'The Son of God loved me, and gave Himself for me'. And there are others."

"Um ... um," said Joyce, "I'm sure that's true, that love means giving. Mind, you haven't to rule out the pleasure you get when you give to someone you love. And it does deepen as well as express the love, doesn't it?"

"Sure, and in religion people have always found that giving is one of the pathways to God's presence. John Dryden said, 'Alms are but the vehicles of prayer'. And I do like the practical suggestion that I came across last week in the Old Testament. It said 'As water quenches a blazing fire, so almsgiving atones for sin'."

"Um ... um," said Joyce again. She was never very happy when I started throwing texts at a subject. "I think you've got to expect much less from Maggie now that she's on her own. You know what they say about two living as cheaply as one; well, she'll still have to pay household expenses just the same, but with only one pension to live on, she'll have quite a struggle, poor thing."

There was no evidence that Maggie intended to restrict her generosity in any way following the funeral of Florrie. In fact, on the very evening of the Service, I found Maggie waiting at the back of the church in the dim light as I made my way out after Evensong. After thanking me for the funeral arrangements, she produced twenty one-pound notes which she pressed into my hand.

"I paid the undertaker this afternoon," she said, "and this is the money left over from the Insurance Policy. Do please use it for some poor person in the parish."

It was on the tip of my tongue to refuse. I wanted to say, "But there are not many people round here poorer than you, Maggie. For goodness sake, keep it and treat yourself to a new coat or a pair of shoes, or what about a chicken for dinner, or maybe a few extra bags of coal?" But I bit my tongue instead, and with just a moment's hesitation accepted the gift. "Thanks," I said, "there's a family with five or six kids which has moved into the parish recently. They're desperate, I know, so I'll use some of it to help them. Thanks again." I knew I had done right. Who was I to interfere in Maggie's relationship with her God? And in any case, I was just beginning to recognise that God's care for people was as practical as mine, and infinitely wiser. My learning was a slow and painful process.

And then it happened again. Maggie's generosity that is. More personal this time and, therefore, harder to accept. It was a week or so later that I discovered in the Vicarage hall a brown paper parcel. Emanating from it was a loud ticking sound that could only come from The Clock. Any doubts were immediately dispelled when the house echoed to a new sound as the hour was loudly proclaimed. I put it under my arm without so much as a peep at it, and returned it whence it came. "If you want us to have it," I explained, "leave it to us in your Will, but keep it in its usual place on the mantelpiece in the meantime."

Maggie was deeply upset; tears came into her eyes. "It's not merely that I want you to have it for what you and Mrs. Brown have done," she said, "but Florrie and I agreed that we wanted it to have a good home after our days, and that as soon as one of us died, the other would ask you to have it. We knew you would value it. Do please accept it ... please."

She was greatly relieved and pleased when I finally capitulated. I promised to take care of it and 'give it a good home'. I had found it very difficult to accept something so personal. It was much easier to give and to do things for others than to receive. Something to do with pride, the deadliest of the deadly sins, I suspected. Yet as I carried the clock home, I found solace in remembering how Jesus was superb at receiving things. No qualms with Him on that score. "The women ministered unto Him of their substance" we are told. He accepted hospitality all the time. He accepted a boy's lunch of five loaves and two small fishes. He borrowed a donkey, an upper room, a boat. Born in a borrowed manger, He was buried in a borrowed tomb. As He died on the Cross He asked for a drink, and begged a home for His mother. Contrary to what I once heard a Sunday School teacher say to her class, "Neither a lender nor a borrower be" does not sum up the teaching of Jesus Christ. The opposite would get close.

"Maggie's blessed clock" we christened it, trying to use it as a reminder of our need to accept as well as give. It is still ticking away in the background as I write these words many years later. The strike is still as loud, the lesson still as vital. Maybe it is as we learn to accept little things in life that we gradually condition ourselves to accept the greatest free gift of all — eternal life, through the forgiveness and love that come from the Cross of Christ. A great Christian teacher has said that "to accept our acceptance" is the most vital step in discipleship. St. Paul puts it more simply: we are "to grow up like Him in all things, unto the measure of the stature of the fulness of Christ," and that must include using our two hands as He did — one for giving, one for receiving. Even the clock uses both its hands in an appropriate way!

CHAPTER SIX

"Let all things be done decently and in order."

(St Paul: 1 Cor 14 v 40)

I wondered why it had been necessary to swear me to secrecy regarding the funeral arrangements. The voice on the telephone had been very insistent. "Just book the date, please, but not a word to anyone. It's very important that you keep it to yourself until we come round and give you more details. Did you say tonight at seven?" I replied in the affirmative.

They were punctual to the minute. A man in his late forties with his two grown-up daughters. All wearing black, obviously very distressed. Both women had red eyes from recent tears, and even as I let them into the house the man was wiping his eyes with a handkerchief as he pretended to blow his nose.

"Do please sit down," I said as soon as we were in the study. "I am sorry to see you so upset. Do please accept my sympathy; losing a loved one is an awful experience, I am very sorry. I promise I'll say a prayer for you."

"Thank you," the man replied. He was thin, looked rather gaunt, had dark receding hair. When he spoke he was a bit hesitant. "Er ... is it arranged then: Tuesday, isn't it, er ... er ... at eleven o'clock?"

I confirmed the details I had agreed earlier with the funeral director. "And after the Service in church," I added, "I believe you would like to go to Overdale Crematorium. I think it's all been fixed up so there are no problems with the arrangements."

He nodded in assent. "We are all very tired," he said wearily. "Only flew in from America this morning, and we've been on the go ever since."

I offered a cup of tea but it was refused. "It's my wife,

116

Cara, who has died, as you know," he said. "Five days ago it happened; it was very sudden. We were actually at a dance together at the Great Britain Club in New York. Heart attack, of course, so distressing. When the ambulance eventually arrived, they wouldn't take her to hospital until we could produce fifty dollars in cash. The people present were marvellous — had a whip-round there and then, but sadly it was too late. She was dead by the time they got her to hospital. Such a beautiful woman, and far too young to die."

There was silence for a few minutes as his handkerchief came out again to wipe his eyes. For the first time one of the daughters spoke as she sought to ease any embarrassment her father might have felt by this display of emotion. "Vicar," she said, "you will be wondering why we asked you to keep the details of the funeral confidential until we had been this evening. Well, you see, my mother was Elvis Presley's housekeeper, and for several years she has been a very close friend of his. He's devastated by her death, and he's been very generous and helpful to us, but he wants to avoid any unnecessary publicity. As you can guess, the press plague him like locusts, and he has to be so careful. You do understand, don't you?"

I said that I did, and waited for more information. The father had recovered sufficiently to take over the conversation once more. "Mr. Presley is meeting all the costs," he said, "and he has told us that everything must be done exactly as my wife would have wished. She was born and brought up in this part of Bolton, and always said that one day she would return and live here again. I never thought she would only return in a box. Oh dear me." He put his head in his hands and started to weep softly.

The same daughter came to the rescue once more. "He really is a nice man, Mr. Presley, so very kind. Do you know, he even chartered a special aeroplane for us to come back to England with mother's body. I couldn't begin to tell you how generous and thoughtful he has been — I don't know

117

what we would have done without him."

I nodded encouragingly. "It's good to hear he's like that," I said. "I don't know a lot about him, but I've seen him on television, of course, and he is certainly very popular. I can understand the need for confidentiality, otherwise your mother's funeral might become even more difficult for you if crowds of pressmen and photographers turned up. But quite honestly, I don't think you have any need to be worried, for no one here will connect the funeral with Elvis Presley, except, of course, the members of your own family. Have you many relatives still in this part of the world?"

"Yes," the man answered, "we are quite a big family on both sides, mine and hers, so I think there will be a lot of people in church for the service. And that brings me to the next thing I want to say." He cleared his throat nervously. "Now Vicar, Mr. Presley has made a special request. He told us to be sure to ask the minister taking the service to play one of his records as part of the ceremony. In fact, he has even given us the one he wants you to play." He felt in his inside pocket and drew out a small single disc. He handed it me across the desk.

I noticed it had a larger than usual hole in the middle, the size of a ten-penny piece. "Which side is the one you are interested in?" I asked as I examined it. By their faces I could see it was the one I was looking at. "I see, so it's this song — 'Crying in the Chapel' — that right?"

"That's it, that's the one Mr. Presley wants played," said the girl. "It's a lovely song and very religious; I'm sure you'll think it's suitable. And I do hope you'll be willing to let it be played in church."

My heart sank through my boots! I hated the thought of cheapening the lovely Prayer Book Service with this kind of thing. It seemed so important to me to let the quiet dignity of the Funeral Service speak its own message with its rare beauty and solemnity. It was only rarely that I interrupted its flow even with an address, and I liked to think it was exactly the same for everybody, king or commoner, rich or poor, sinner or saint. As the years went by, I was to learn that it is possible to combine the formal and the informal, and to value the introduction of more personal things into this type of situation. But I was not at the stage yet, and my brain was working overtime to find some sort of compromise.

"This record won't fit a normal machine as it is," I said, "but I think I can stick a circle of cardboard in the middle, and then it will be usable on an English record-player. I'll be pleased to do that for you, of course, so that it will fit the splendid equipment they use at the crematorium. We could play it after the committal, just before we leave the chapel. Would make a nice end to the whole Service, don't you think?"

The three of them glanced at one another. There was alarm, even dismay, in their looks. The same girl expressed their fears. "Oh no, Vicar, please! I know we are making an unusual request but Mr. Presley said he wanted to feel he was making a definite contribution to the actual Service in church, and he hoped his song would come immediately after the Reading from the Bible." She looked at me pleadingly.

"OK, we'll have it in church," I replied, but then I made a last attempt to limit the damage. "How about letting Elvis Presley set the tone of the whole thing by hearing from him at the very beginning? Then the rest of the Order can be followed in the usual way without interruption." I could see my rather feeble attempt at casuistry had failed by their crestfallen expressions. I gave in as gracefully as I could.

"I get the impression you don't like that idea either. Right, I'll play the record exactly where he wanted it; I'm sure it will be very nice." I tried to make it sound sincere but I still had a deep feeling of unease, hoping it would not cheapen a solemn occasion and, even more, that it would not set a dangerous precedent.

It was in that frame of mind that I found myself four days later walking down the aisle in front of the American

119

casket in which the body had been brought to this country. As we processed through the building, the glorious words of the Opening Sentences were on my lips: "I am the Resurrection and the Life, saith the Lord; he that believeth in me, though he were dead, yet shall he live: and whosoever liveth and believeth in me shall never die."

The service was under way. Hymn, prayers, Bible Reading came in quick succession. Then came the special moment. Standing in the clergy stall I announced, "Will the congregation please remain seated while we have some special music." There had to be no mention of the connection of the family with the pop star. I bent down to the floor to the record-player and pressed the switch. As the music started, I was glad to disappear two paces backwards behind the Chancel arch, for this was one way of sparing my blushes as the mushy sentimental song started to echo through the church. Though I was not enamoured of his music, I was very impressed by Elvis' care and generosity. He had promised that on the day of the funeral, he would get up early, find a quiet place, and join us in spirit. He had been given over the phone the precise details, and the knowledge that he was doing this was greatly comforting to them all. Maybe the thing he wanted to say to them particularly came near the end of his song. The voice boomed out:

Take your troubles to the chapel,
Get down on your knees and pray,
Then your burden will be lightened,
And you'll surely find the way.

At the end of the song the machine switched itself off with a click. I breathed a sigh of relief and reappeared, quickly ushering things back into the normal Anglican decorum with, "Let us pray". Everybody knelt, and we were back into the familiar pattern. The old prayers had never sounded lovelier.

Soon we were off to the crematorium with the headlights

120

of hearse, taxis and cars all switched on — another Americanism that had been requested, and then finally came the time when I stood in the foyer, everything completed, shaking hands with the mourners as they filed out of the chapel to their cars for the homeward journey. After the family came those friends and neighbours of former years who lived locally, some of them my parishioners. Mrs. Hawke was practically the last to emerge. A small tubby woman in her sixties, she lived in the same street as my church and was nicknamed 'Whispering Grass' because of the hoarse low voice she possessed. I could tell she had something on her mind by the excited look in her eyes. She grabbed my arm and steered me into a corner. "Eh Vicar," she said, "I sat in church with Mrs. Jenkins and we couldn't get over how well you sang that song." I was taken by surprise and rendered speechless for a few moments. The grating voice continued: "I don't want to tell you your job, but I will say this, if you sang one or two songs like that every Sunday, more people would come to church, I can tell you." I bit hard on my lip, shook her hand, and went into the office to sign the book.

"You will be able to dine out on that one," quipped Joyce across the table at lunch-time as she enjoyed the story and offered to buy me a guitar for Christmas. The simple meal tasted good, made better by the calm-after-the-storm feeling I was experiencing. All in all, the funeral had not been as hard to cope with as I had imagined, and another difficult thing was out of the way. I was on my second cup of tea when the phone rang.

"Always the same," grumbled Joyce, "you never get a meal in peace. Leave it — whoever it is will call back if it's important." I sat there feeling guilty as I sipped my tea. The ringing persisted; I finally surrendered, rushed to the study and picked up the phone.

It was a woman's voice with a broad Bolton accent. Seemed like a routine call to arrange yet another funeral. "Mi dad died this morning, and we want t'funeral at St Thomas's."

"Certainly," I replied, "I'm sorry to hear about your dad, and if there is anything I can do you've only to say the word. I'll be glad to help in any way I can."

"Yes, we know that," said the woman, "that's why I'm phoning you. We like the way you do 'em, otherwise we'd have gone to the Methodists."

"Er ... er ... well, thanks, yes. Now, if you'll give me your address I'll come and see you so that we can arrange all the details. That's better than trying to do it by telephone."

"Might be better if we came and saw you, don't you think? Then we could bring the gramophone records at t'same time."

Good Lord, I thought, not again! Lightning cannot strike twice in the same place in such a short time. I suddenly felt weak at the knees as I edged round the desk and dropped into the chair at the back. I had to make a conscious effort to bring my voice down an octave before I posed the inevitable question. "Records! What records?"

"Well it's not Elvis Presley, you'll be pleased to hear, none of us like 'im; it's something much more appropriate. All the family are here; we've been discussing it; all very upset, and

122

we feel we need help. So that's it.''

"I'm not with you; what do you mean, 'that's it'?"

"'Help!'" said the woman. "You know, it's a song sung by the Beatles, and it sums up just how we all feel. You must know it. 'Help me if you can I'm feeling do-o-o-wn'," she expanded; "'And I do appreciate you being ro-o-o-und: Help me get my feet back on the gro-o-o-und, Won't you ple-e-ase help me'. Now, don't you think that's lovely? Could anything be nicer?"

I put a hand to my forehead in despair and could feel the perspiration beginning to ooze out. The voice went on for a few minutes extolling the virtues of the Beatles, but I was not listening. I was having a quick complaining session with God. I did not exactly say, "This is another fine mess you've got me into," but that was the gist of it, as I expressed my disappointment that every time I tried to be charitable and compassionate, I seemed to get clobbered for it. It was one of the many times before and since when I have felt a great affinity with St. Teresa of Avila. After a series of misadventures whilst striving to serve the Lord, she told God that if that was the way He treated His friends, she was not surprised He had so few of them!

I tuned in again to the voice on the phone. I could hardly believe what came next. "And since mi dad's worked all his life for the Town Council, we thought it would be nice to have a kind of musical appreciation for his contribution to the community."

The alarm-bells were ringing furiously in my head in time with my accelerated heart beats. I still could not believe that the chickens had come home to roost with such a vengeance. "Oh yes," I croaked, "what had you in mind?"

"Well, he was 'on the bins' for more than twenty years, so we thought it would be lovely if, half-way through the Service in church, we could have Lonnie Donegan singing, 'My Old Man's A Dustman'. That really would make it so personal and moving, don't you agree?"

123

"I certainly don't agree," I exploded. This was just too bizarre for words. I knew I could not prevaricate any longer, my foot had to be put down very firmly indeed.

"I'm sorry," I said, and I was aware that I was almost shouting, "I'm very sorry, but I cannot allow any of this. It's a parish church I'm running, not a discotheque. You can play those records at home either before or after the Funeral Service, but they are certainly not suitable for a place of worship. I hope I make myself absolutely clear!"

There was a bellow of rage from the other end of the line. "How dare you say that!" the woman demanded with a shout. "What's the difference between the Beatles and Elvis Presley? Tell me that! Or is it money you're after? Well, we'll pay. What sort of a backhander did they have to give you for Elvis today?" she taunted. The tirade continued with, "I'll bet you're one of those who makes fish of one and flesh of another, aren't you; but I'll report this to the Bishop. I'll tell him you pretend to help people and then let them down when it comes to the crunch. It's hypocrisy, that's what it is, sheer hypocrisy! I don't know how you can for shame wear that collar."

I was very agitated so I took a deep breath and tried to speak slowly and calmly; I turned the volume down too. "Look, it's no good our falling out over this, and I will try to help you, but there's no way I'm having the Beatles and a skiffle-group singer performing at a funeral in church. That's absolutely final, and you can report me to the Bishop, the Archbishop, and even the Pope, if you like, but I'm just not having it."

I seemed to be getting the message across for there was a subdued response. "Oh ... I see ... right." I could hear a mumbled conversation taking place at the other end involving several voices.

I began to feel a bit guilty, shouting like that, and at a woman recently bereaved. I got out the oil-can for the troubled waters. "Look, why not come and see me tonight so that we can have a cup of tea together and a chat? We can discuss the whole thing in a calm and sensible way.''

"Do you mean you might change your mind, and let us, at least, have, 'My Old Man's A Dustman'?''

I was back in top gear in a trice. "Certainly not! Please get that firmly into your head; no funny songs, no pop music, nothing like that at all. Do you understand? There was a very special reason for the Elvis Presley song being used in church this morning. I cannot tell you what it was, but as I say, it was a very special reason indeed.''

"Oh yes? Tell that to the Marines! Whose leg do you think you are pulling? Oh, that's a good one! I like that. Whose leg do you think you are pulling?'' To my astonishment there followed a burst of laughter that went on for nearly a minute.

I was beginning to wonder whether the woman had gone mad, or perhaps was getting hysterical, when she managed to contain herself sufficiently to speak again: "Vicar, there's somebody here who wants a word.''

The penny was beginning to drop even before I heard Cliff's voice. He was one of the sidesmen and a good friend. "You're never going to forgive me for this, Vicar, are you? but you can blame Jack as well; he's here too.'' I could hear more laughter in the background. Cliff continued, "And you must admit, this girl in the office here is a great actress, deserves an Oscar for her performance, even though we did rehearse her thoroughly before the curtain went up.''

Anger and relief vied with each other in my mind, but the latter quickly got on top, assisted as it was with the need to appear a good sport. But I was still smarting a little as I said, "You rotters, what a dirty trick! I suppose I should have twigged it earlier, for there's no doubt 'My Old Man's A Dustman' was a bit over the top, but in this job you can't really be surprised at anything, and I was at a big disadvantage talking to somebody who was supposedly just bereaved. But go on, enjoy your joke. I know there'll be plenty of laughter over your pints tonight in the 'Bowling Green' won't there?''

"Shouldn't think so,'' he replied quickly but without

conviction. Then he added, "But I was a bit surprised how easy it was to pull the wool over your eyes. After all Vicar, you are supposed to be a professional in that area. But anyway, thanks for taking it so well — see you tonight at the meeting — bye."

I put the phone down and went back to the dining-room with the un-Christian thought that it would be lovely to get my own back. I could not readily think of anything that would bring revenge, but I knew that if the opportunity presented itself, I would not be slow to grasp it. I said as much to Joyce.

"I thought it was your business to teach people to forgive," she reminded me with mock solemnity. "Isn't it seventy-times-seven or something before you're even allowed to consider having a swipe back?"

"Sometimes I'm a supporter of the Old Testament philosophy," I replied, "you know, 'an eye for an eye, and a tooth for a tooth'."

"Take your tongue out of your cheek," she said, "or you'll not be able to say your prayers properly at Evensong."

One prayer I did say properly that evening was a penitential one for having so quickly blamed God for the recent crisis. Then came the Psalms and the Prayers and the Bible Readings. Through them it was often possible to apologise, grumble, complain, argue, listen, ask a favour, express gratitude, even be lifted up in adoration and praise. Some times more than others, of course, for the relationship with God for most people tends to blow hot and cold. Yet even on the coldest day, there is a satisfaction in accepting the tedium of worship as a way of making an offering to God and of witnessing to Him. It is not unknown to discover with hindsight that rare spiritual fruits germinate at very low temperatures. At the end of Evensong I locked the church and moved next door to the school where a meeting had been arranged to review our plans for our Annual Sermons' Day.

This was a major event in the life of the parish, always held on the second Sunday in May, dating back to before the turn of the century. Many northern parishes had a similar festival, often for the same purpose, namely to focus attention on and raise money for the Day and Sunday Schools in a parish. Originally, visiting preachers were expected to preach sermons on this subject — hence the name for this special day — and although the ethos had changed, the children themselves were still given a prominent place in the proceedings.

Two great Processions were at the heart of the day, morning and afternoon, and large numbers of youngsters were involved, walking behind banners, tableaux, the Rose Queens and with the uniformed organisations. Each time, two professional brass bands accompanied the walkers, among whom were many adults, encouraged to take advantage of the opportunity to make an act of witness to their Christian commitment and church membership. Hundreds of spectators lined the streets, smiling and waving, as the walkers went by. At certain places we would stop and sing a hymn, led by the large robed choir in our midst. All the time, a dozen or so of the men of the parish moved among the spectators with collecting-tins, and there was always much gaiety and fun about the whole affair.

Each Procession ended outside the church, when walkers and watchers streamed in for a special service. In spite of the large size of the building with its 800 seats, extra chairs were always needed, and even this provision did not cater for the late-comers who had to sit on the floor or stand wherever there was an inch of space. A special choir of about fifty or so children, all dressed in white and known as the 'Little Singers', was positioned on the Chancel steps, trained to perform their particular musical items as well as augment the singing that came from the usual choir in the Chancel. Unlike the great Christian festivals of Christmas and Easter, Sermons' Day was rightly seen as a great celebration of the local church, providing an opportunity for rejoicing in grass-roots Christianity, with its friendships, mutual support, multifarious activities, and enrichment of life for so many. You could take your pick from football to chess; from flower-arranging to

127

drama; from tennis to DIY; from visiting the sick to taking the youngsters on camp; from painting pictures to painting the gutters. Amidst all the variety, the unifying factor was the parish church itself, for the members of the organisations which catered for everybody from toddlers to octogenarians, were expected to be members of the worshipping community. When Sermons' Day approached, it was natural that the spotlight should fall on the one place where most of us came together week by week.

The church was scrubbed, polished, decorated and titivated for a full fortnight before the great day itself. Men and women of all ages, shapes and sizes, were encouraged and persuaded into taking part in a mammoth spring-clean that left the building looking its absolute best. The purpose was not so much to enhance its appearance as to express, in a very practical way, an appreciation of the intrinsic experience associated with a place easily and naturally thought of as 'God's House'. What was being done was an act of service to God Himself, and scrubbing and praying merged into one. The church had a sacramental significance, that is it was "an outward and visible sign of an inward and spiritual grace"; the grace being no less a thing than the Divine Presence itself. The occasional jibe that people were being encouraged to worship bricks and mortar was as superficial and undeserved as to say they were also encouraged to worship bread and wine. God's "otherness" and His "nearness" came together in this place. "Yea, we can", they sang with sincerity as well as gusto in one of their favourite hymns:

> Thou who art beyond the farthest
>   Mortal eye can scan,
> Can it be that thou regardest
>   Songs of sinful man?
> Can we know that thou art near us,
>   And wilt hear us?
>   Yea, we can.

It was the smell of Sermons' Day that fascinated me. Absolutely distinctive, and any person connected with the parish would have been able to recognise it a mile off. A curious mixture of soap and disinfectant, paint and varnish, polish and flowers; here separate, there mingled, but all in all the unmistakable aroma of this special day. But even the smell, with its constituent parts, was a reminder of the various elements that had to be brought together, if the tradition of a happy and successful occasion was to be maintained. A small committee of a dozen or so members had again been appointed to oversee the arrangements.

I was the last to arrive in the classroom where our deliberations were to take place. Even in the hubbub of conversation, I was able to identify a tune being whistled by the two men near the door as I went in, but 'My Old Man's A Dustman' fizzled out as huge grins on the faces of Cliff and Jack made further whistling impossible. I tried to return the grins, said a prayer, and got the meeting under way. A smile would have come more easily to my lips had I been aware that events were unfolding which would, at least, go some way to make up for my having been made to look something of an idiot. Quickly and efficiently, the key people present assumed responsibility for different aspects of the arrangements, and then we divided into groups under a leader for a more detailed analysis of the situation in a particular area.

Cliff was by trade a painter and decorator, so naturally took charge of that side of things. He was soon allocating particular tasks to those in the group. Walter and I were asked to re-varnish the main door; Jack Crook and Tom would touch up the French polish on the oak panelling; two others had the job of painting the gates and the railings; Cliff himself, assisted by Jack, would repaint the heating grids on the floor down the sides of the centre aisle. These fretwork iron grids covered the 4″ heating pipes that lay in ducts below the surface. They were always painted black which was very convenient for, as

Walter reminded us, we had been given a gallon of black paint some months before by a former parishioner. I had stored it in the attic at the Vicarge.

Walter had a basic rule that anything offered to the church should never be refused. He believed this was one way of conferring dignity upon the donor: my attic bore testimony to the practical implications of his philosophy. It was an Aladdin's cave full of Walteralia. The heaviest thing I had helped to carry up there recently was an old iron mangle, known locally as a "pair of squeezers". It had taken its place alongside six double beds, a metal bath, a harmonium, a three-piece suite, sundry chairs, rugs, and rolled-up carpets. Pictures large and small leaned against the walls, and there was a rusty, foul-smelling gas geyser half blocking the doorway. My hopes of a workbench up there never quite left me, but grew fainter and fainter.

It was good to be taking something out of the place for a change. I climbed up the stairs to get the paint. As I picked it up, I glanced around once more for the pint of engine-oil I had searched for before. The donor of the paint had tied a luggage label round the handle, listing the three or four things he had given, and all were accounted for except the oil. I suspected that maybe we had failed to pick it up initially, or perhaps it had got lost in transit. It was of little consequence, so I tore up the label and carried the paint to church.

It was put to good use straight away. Part of it was poured into a spare can and then, kneeling on prayer hassocks, Cliff and Jack took a side each, and started to work their way down the aisle. With all the nooks and crannies of the fretwork in the metal, it was slow work, but they were both expert with a brush, and I stood for a while watching the rusty, chipped metal being transformed inch by inch. As I went to continue my own job, Cliff gave me a message for Walter: "Tell him that for once, somebody has given him something that is actually useful — drop of good stuff this paint — wonders never cease!''

Before we went home for the night, another smell joined the other pungent odours of the church, that of fish and chips liberally sprinkled with vinegar, eaten in their papers in the porch, the traditional item on the menu of the celebratory feast that marked the end of the "fourteen days hard labour". It simply remained now for the ladies to do their stuff with the dozen or so flower displays that added the final touches to our preparations. With two full days to go, they had ample time to make their contribution before the arrival of our special day.

It was Friday evening before I suspected that something might be wrong. The ladies had obviously made a start with the flowers, for by the time I went to Evensong some of the basic things had already been completed, and they were clearly ready for the big push the following day. What was less reassuring were the black paint smudges on the brown lino of the centre aisle, obviously coming from the freshly-painted grids. It was but a few minutes' job to remove them with turps and a cloth, but I took the precaution of leaving all the doors open to hasten the drying process when I returned to the Vicarage for my Friday evening surgery. It was getting on for ten o'clock before I was able to get back again and lock the church doors. I felt sure the current of air going through the building would have made all the difference. Alas, I was wrong.

Saturday Evensong was delayed for more than an hour while the Curate and I — augmented by some hastily summoned assistants — tried to clear up the awful mess we had discovered when we arrived. It was clear that lots of people had, as usual, visited the church to see the flowers and the result of the spring-clean; it was clear too that they had traipsed their way to the four corners of the church with wet paint on their shoes. It was bad enough coping with the mess, but even as we restored the floor to its pristine glory, we were very apprehensive at the thought of hundreds and hundreds of pairs of feet in the place, and we bitterly thought of the morrow!

The following morning, everything was done that could be done. The paint was still as fluid and fresh as the moment it was applied, and an attempt was made to prevent anyone making contact with it by having a line of upended chairs down the length of the aisle on each side, leaving a narrow space in the centre for people to walk in safety. It worked well for the early Communion Service, but was bound to fail when people rushed in after the two Processions. Many pairs of white shoes and socks were ruined as children pushed and shoved to get into their places. The white dresses that emerged without a spot or two of paint were the exception, and even the retiring Rose Queen's train managed to acquire a set of black fingerprints that did little to enhance its claim to be regal attire. Some of the children were actually in tears, though there were many smiles too, from young and old, with the biggest, I thought, on the face of Leonard James, who ran a dry-cleaning business on Halliwell Road!

We ended the final Service of the day in the usual way with the popular hymn, "The day Thou gavest Lord, is ended", and I stood at the door with my "Goodnights" laced with apologies and commiserations. There were few if any complaints, most people seeing the funny side of the affair, but by the time they had all gone, I realised I had a golden opportunity to extract at least something positive from what had been a very worrying day. By this time I had fathomed the mystery and knew exactly what had caused the disaster, but I kept my own counsel as I made my way into the Vestry to remove my robes and join the men who were there counting the collection. The Churchwardens were at it, assisted as usual by Cliff and Jack.

I put on a grave face as I entered. "Bad news," I said, "I'm afraid this is going to be a messy business in more ways than one." Turning to Cliff I asked: "Your full name is Clifford, isn't it?" Then with a glance at his companion, "Now your

132

name is, I think, John, isn't it, even though we call you Jack?".
They nodded in agreement but looked surprised. "I'm glad
I've got it right — that's what I've told them at the back of
the church," I said.

"What's all this about?" Cliff asked.

"There's a group of people in church asking for the full
names of those responsible for today's calamity," I said,
"they're making notes and taking photographs. Planning
some kind of legal action, I understand."

"How ridiculous!" exclaimed Cliff. "All they need do is
take their things to the cleaners."

"As a matter of fact they mentioned the cleaners," I said,
"but I'm afraid it wasn't their clothes they were thinking of.
They've just told me it's you and Jack they hope to take there.
Said they are going to sue you — not only for the damage
you've caused but for the distress to them and their children."

Cliff spoke: "Isn't it really the church that's liable, rather
than the two of us? Doesn't the 'Third Party Insurance' Policy
cover this kind of thing?" He was beginning to look rather
worried.

"Doubt it," I replied, "I'll get it out when I get home and
read it carefully, but I rather think, speaking from memory,
that it doesn't cover the gross negligence of particular
individuals."

"Gross negligence!" they exclaimed together like an
explosion. Then Cliff said, "How do you make that out? We
were only doing our best."

"Will you please come into the church and meet these
people?" I invited. "There are about twenty of them, and
I must warn you, they seem to be in an ugly mood. So take
my advice, and apologise. Admit liability, and say that you'll
make proper compensation."

"I'm not doing that," said Cliff. They both looked cowed
and uncomfortable as they straightened their ties and got ready
to go with me. "I'm afraid you were responsible," I said,
"after all, the paint you used was specially doctored so that

it would never dry — you know, it's used on drain-pipes and gutters to deter burglars.'' Surprise was written all over their faces as I continued, imparting the information that had come from my sub-conscious half-an-hour before at the end of the Service. I now knew exactly what the message on the label had meant when it said, 'Six cups and saucers; a bucket; a gallon of black paint plus one pint of engine oil'! I could have kicked myself for not twigging it earlier. I continued with, ''I understand you add engine-oil to paint to achieve that effect; right, Cliff? After all, you are supposed to be a professional in this area, aren't you?''

I was surprised my last sentence did not immediately open their eyes, but the woebegone expression stayed with them. I tried again. ''You must have known, Cliff; I can't believe it would be all that easy to pull the wool over your eyes, for as I say, you are supposed to be a professional in that area, aren't you.'' As their faces told me they were beginning to take it in, I clinched it with, ''And that girl in your office isn't the only one who should be awarded an Oscar, is she?''

''I knew from the start you were joking,'' said Cliff, but there was a relief in his voice that belied his words. ''You knew it too, Jack, didn't you?'' Jack, who had gone back to counting the collection, winked and smiled as he pretended to wipe the sweat from his brow. The Churchwardens had worked on throughout the conversation without batting an eyelid; they had known exactly what was going on. Both shrewd men, one would have to get up very early indeed to catch them out.

Cliff lived near me and we walked home together. I knew there was a question he was dying to ask. It came just before we parted. ''Vicar,'' he said, ''surely you didn't plan the whole thing ... did you? You wouldn't go to such lengths to get even, would you? I mean ... you didn't actually put the oil in the ...''

I put on an enigmatic smile that would have done credit to the Mona Lisa. ''That would be telling,'' I said with a laugh, but I did feel flattered that he thought me remotely capable of such a diabolical deed. Mind, I knew I really was responsible, for I should have read that wretched label properly and with more intelligence. I continued to pay the price for my negligence by spending the next two nights, with Cliff and Jack, wiping the paint off the grids. It was a filthy job, but there was no alternative.

I had decided that if 'My Old Man's A Dustman' was whistled or sung, I would retaliate with 'I'm painting the clouds with sunshine'. Not very apposite, I knew, but the best I could come up with. As it turned out, I did not need to use it. "You're a rum blighter for a Vicar," said Cliff as we finished the cleaning-up operation. "Do you reckon we're about equal with each other now?" –

Basking in undeserved glory, I said I thought the score was about even. "'Quits' is the word that comes to mind," I observed with a laugh. He headed for the 'Bowling Green' for a pint. I headed for the Vicarage, for I wanted to catch the nine o'clock news on television.

As it happened, I heard the headlines only, for at that stage Walter arrived with a request. "I'm uneasy about Miss Taylor," he began, "and I wondered whether you would be kind enough to run me over to her house. So sorry to bother you, but like they say, 'There's no rest for the wicked'."

I groaned inwardly for I was tired, but agreed. "Go and tell Joyce what we are up to," I said, "she's in the lounge. And while you're doing it, I'll go and get the car out."

Miss Taylor lived two or three miles away on the other side of town. I was thinking about her as I went to the garage. One of Walter's protégées, she was a remarkable old lady well in her eighties. At one time, she had been headmistress of a large school in Bolton, and had become a good friend of the Reverend Joseph Bridgman, one of my predecessors as Vicar of St. Thomas'. This is how she had come to meet Walter. Now ailing and rather eccentric, she was one of the many lame ducks in his care.

I parked the car by the Vicarage gate, waiting for Walter to join me. Although tired, I was looking forward to seeing the old dame again for she was a lively character whom I much admired. I knew, sadly, she was beginning to fail mentally and physically, for she was certainly neglecting her nice home. She had developed some rather eccentric habits too, like never going to bed. She slept in a chair downstairs in front of the fire, and strongly resisted all efforts to change this. Oddly enough, she also retained a great interest in soccer, persuading Walter whenever possible to take her to watch Bolton Wanderers at Burnden Park. She was a very enthusiastic supporter, cheering and booing at least as loudly as anybody else in the crowd, and I was astonished on more than one occasion to see this nicely-dressed, demure old lady leap to her feet and use her faultless diction to berate an unfortunate referee whenever he happened to make a decision with which she disagreed. "A pair of glasses, Sir, that's what you need," she would cry, and taking it a stage further, she had been known to demand in stentorian tones, "Where's your white stick today, Mr. Referee? Yes, your white stick?"

Walter got into the car with a question on his lips. "Joyce tells me you talked to the specialist today about Miss Taylor — did you get anywhere?"

"No. Told him we were worried about her, and asked whether he could get her into hospital for a check-up and a rest."

"And?"

"Told me to mind my own business. Wouldn't discuss the case. Sarcastic and rude: 'You look after their souls', he said, 'and leave their bodies to me. I get fed up with people meddling in things they know nothing about'. I would have slammed the phone down on him, but unfortunately he did it first. I was flippin' annoyed, I can tell you. Pompous ass!"

Walter nodded sympathetically. We were arriving in the affluent part of the town where Miss Taylor lived. She had a nice detached house between the Chief Constable's and the Borough Pathologist's. Across the road was the private home of a wealthy hotelier. One of the old lady's regular jokes was to say, 'With my neighbours, I can be locked up, cut up, or put up!' She was not in a joking mood on this occasion, however, and in fact looked poorly and frail as she welcomed us into her home, though her charm and hospitality, so deeply engrained in her character, had not deserted her.

"Do sit down," she said, "and make yourself comfortable while I make you some tea." She disappeared into the kitchen.

Walter groaned. "Oh no," he said, "please don't let it be cream-crackers again!" He had often told me of his aversion to this type of biscuit, and of Miss Taylor's conviction that he ought to eat them because they were good for him. She invariably plastered them with a thick coating of cheap margarine which was another reason for Walter's distaste.

It seemed to take her a long time, but eventually she reappeared with a tea trolley. I saw at a glance that Walter's worst fears were realised! I knew the biscuit was for him, for in reply to a question called from the kitchen, I had declined food of any kind.

"There, Walter, one of your favourites; you eat that while I pour the tea," she said as she handed him the biscuit on a plate. Then turning to me she said, "He neglects himself, needs building up."

I saw Walter pick up the *Bolton Evening News* that was lying on a side-table. Sitting alongside, I could see his every movement. The newspaper was held in front of him as though he were engrossed in the contents, but behind its cover the cream-cracker was folded into two halves. I admired the dexterity of his left hand as, having accomplished the difficult manoeuvre, the two halves were stuck together with the margarine and then eased towards his top pocket. Half of it had disappeared inside when Miss Taylor came to his side with a cup of tea.

"Walter! Walter! What on earth are you doing with that cream-cracker?" she demanded.

He was completely taken aback for a few seconds. His face reddened as he grinned sheepishly. "Er ... er ... well ... it's like this ... I thought it would be nice to have it later on ... at home for supper ... I was sort of saving it for later."

He found it difficult to produce a lie, even when it was as white as driven snow.

"You silly boy," said the old lady who could transform herself into a headmistress at the drop of a hat, "you silly boy. Eat it now. I've plenty of them. There, I'll butter you another one." That too landed on his plate. Two more were duly smothered with a quarter-inch coating of marge. "I'll get a bag from the kitchen," she said, "and then you will be able to take these home for supper." This done, she wagged a finger in his face with the admonition that he must not forget to eat them. "It's the fibre in them you need, the fibre; you do understand?"

She watched like a hawk while poor Walter munched his way through them, though he did manage a surreptitious grimace in my direction once or twice. On the way back, he was more convinced than ever that she needed a period of care and rest in hospital. "I don't think she's capable of washing herself properly at present," he said, "and you can guess the main ingredient in her diet! I don't like the idea, but I think I'll have to have a go at that geriatric consultant tomorrow. I could get out of work for half-an-hour at lunchtime; might catch him then. Mind if I use your phone?"

Walter worked at Burton's Clothing Factory as a clerk in the warehouse. It was within easy distance of the Vicarage. The following day he sat at my desk having dialled the doctor's number. I sat on the edge of the desk, half hoping there would be no reply! But the dialling sound stopped as the instrument was picked up at the other end. "Doctor Selby's office; how can I help you?" It was the same receptionist I had spoken to the day before. I too put my ear near the instrument.

Walter's voice was always a bit squeaky and highpitched, particularly when he got excited, but never more so than now. "Put me through to the doctor, please," he stammered, "this is Walter Ashworth from St. Thomas's."

"St. Thomas's," she repeated, "certainly, Sir, I'll put you through to the doctor right away." I was surprised at the courteous response.

I hardly recognised Dr. Selby's voice when he came on. "Nice to hear from you, Mr. Ashworth," he began with unexpected warmth, "now what can I do for you?"

The gushing friendliness was harder to cope with than the rudeness he had expected. Walter's voice went higher and his words came out with a staccato effect: "Miss Taylor, Belmont Road; friend of mine; what do you make of her?"

"Just a moment, Mr. Ashworth, I'll get her notes." After a short pause the suave voice continued: "Ah yes, here we are; her heart failure has worsened and she now has symptoms of exertional dyspnoea, orthopnea and paroxysmal nocturnal dyspnoea. Her ECG shows a left axis deviation and left bundle branch block, and her chest X-Ray shows significant cardiomegaly and some pulmonary oedema. She also has a megaloblastic anaemia which has been caused by her poor diet. Not a very reassuring picture, I'm afraid."

I now latched on to things and knew exactly what was happening, though Walter remained in blissful ignorance. The doctor and his secretary had interpreted "St. Thomas's" to mean the famous London hospital, and obviously thought they were speaking to an important doctor from the metropolis. I held my breath, wondering what on earth would happen next.

Walter's eyes were bulging in astonishment at the deluge he had unleashed. He coughed into the phone a couple of times, clearing his throat, as he played for time. Finally he came up with, "Oh aye, I see;" then with an unconscious irony: "don't like the sound of all that. But I want to say that in my opinion Miss Taylor should be in hospital right away; today if possible."

He had by a miracle said exactly the right thing, neither too much nor too little.

"I think the same, really," was the response from the doctor

I suspected of being something of a toady. "The problem is a bed; we are very short, as you can guess, but leave it with me; I'll move heaven and earth to get her in. May take a day or so, but have no fears, it will be done."

"Nice of you, and it's been a pleasure talking to you. Thanks very much." Walter put down the phone still in a state of shock, but looking mightily pleased with the way things had gone. I explained what I thought had happened. "Aye, now you mention it, that would explain everything. But I always say I'm from St. Thomas's. First time it's had that effect. Let's just hope it does the trick."

It did. Within twenty-four hours Miss Taylor was comfortably settled in the General Hospital. Quite ill when admitted, but the bed rest and the nutritious food did her the world of good. There had been a few initial protests but then she started to enjoy the experience. In fact, she was positively beaming when I called to see her after a few days. Sitting up in bed and looking much better, she was laying down the law to all and sundry. "I've been having a word with the ward sister," she explained, "and I've told her to be kinder and more considerate to the nurses here; after all, they're only young girls. And I've sent for the hospital secretary too; I want a word about the wages they get — ridiculously low; something must be done about it." I could see she was in great form.

While she was away from home, Walter arranged for some decorating and cleaning to be done. Miss Taylor gave her permission on one condition — that her bedroom had to be emptied of furniture for she intended to continue sleeping downstairs on her return. This demand seemed to give her the guarantee she wanted, and Walter had no option but to comply.

Six weeks later, quite transformed, she was home. To celebrate, Walter took her to watch the Wanderers at Burnden Park. He told me afterwards how much she had enjoyed it. Her observations to the referee had never been more vigorous.

After giving a penalty to the opposition he had ventured to her side of the ground a few minutes later. "Woof, woof," she had called, "woof, woof; your guide dog needs feeding, Sir; woof, woof."

The only negative side of the whole episode was to be found in my attic! A joiner-made pine dressing table with bed to match now lay in the doorway alongside the geyser. A bedside cabinet in the same set with two bedroom chairs were piled on top. It was a work of art to thread one's way through. The possibility of a workbench there providing an oasis for the pursuit of my hobby had taken a pace backwards. And I dreaded what would happen if ever I had to move from the parish. I knew I would be expected to leave the Vicarage completely empty for my successor. I just hoped the problem would never arise.

CHAPTER SEVEN

"All things must change
To something new, to something strange."
(Henry Longfellow, 1807-1882)

An invitation to morning coffee sounded innocent enough, but the fact it came from the Bishop made me apprehensive. I suspected the motive was not the pleasure of my company.

I sat there in his study nibbling a digestive and sipping a cup of instant, waiting for the cards to be put on the table. Dr. William Greer, Bishop of Manchester, was sizing me up from behind his desk. In his mid sixties, he was a tall, slim man, distinguished looking, even handsome, his silver-grey hair parted in the middle and brushed straight back. Even though he had been Principal of Westcott House, one of the country's top theological colleges, he had never learnt the art of small talk. I knew the pleasantries would be kept to a minimum and that we would soon be down to the nitty-gritty.

There was a stillness about him, and a quietness, that singled him out from those who needed to be noticed and admired. He sat back in his chair, his long thin fingers extended and motionless on the desk top in front of him.

"Brace yourself," he said kindly. He had a remarkable ability to be gentle and firm at the same time. "Now then, I wanted to see you this morning because I would like you to become Rector and Rural Dean of Ashton-under-Lyne." He paused, and I saw a faint smile appear as he noticed my look of surprise and alarm. "Do you know where the place is?" he enquired.

I swallowed hard before replying. "Er ... well ... no, not exactly, but isn't it seven or eight miles from Manchester city-centre?: I've never been there. But, forgive me Bishop, why me?"

His nod indicated that he accepted the validity of the question. "Well, the simple answer is that after a great deal of thought, and discussion with members of my Staff, I think you're the right man for the job. And also, I think you've been long enough at Halliwell; nine years is about right; for the proper development of your ministry you ought to move. Now, put those two things together and there you are — in that chair."

I was too stunned to think of anything wise or relevant to say. I sat back to let it sink in as the Bishop gave me a brief sketch of the parish of Ashton, indicating the way he hoped it would be developed in the years ahead. I was hardly taking it in. Rather I was thinking of the shock Joyce and the children would have on my return.

Before I left, however, I was on the receiving end of another shock myself. It was as I stood up ready to depart. The Bishop came round from his desk and stood alongside. "By the way," he said, "please do not misunderstand what I have been saying. I am not asking you to change parishes — I'm telling you! Unless you can honestly say that such a move would have a very bad effect on your family, you have to go. I know leaving Halliwell will be extremely hard, so I'm making it easy for you by giving you an episcopal order." The gentle smile eliminated the peremptoriness of the words without in any way negating them. A good example of his firmness and gentleness working in harmony to produce the right effect.

At any rate I came out knowing I was not simply a pawn in a game of Diocesan chess, played to keep the draughtboard neat and tidy. Thought and care for parish and priest were evident in what he had said. And it was in a peaceful frame of mind that I drove home, in spite of the excitement. There was no "shall-I, shall-I-not" syndrome to be faced, no tossing and turning through sleepless nights. Much simpler than that. I just had to pack up and go.

The thought of the attic flashed into my mind but was

quickly dismissed as the least of my worries. I had no qualms about Joyce either, for I knew she would not make a song and dance about moving, even though she dearly loved our present home and friends.

The children would be a different kettle of fish. Mark at sixteen, Janet at thirteen, would have to face a new home, new schools, new friends, new everything. Moves of this kind are only one of the special problems that clergy children have to face. Janet immediately attacked the cause of the crisis — the poor Bishop. "He is a wicked man," she declared, "he can't move us, this is our home, where we live; I hate Bishops, they're monsters, and I'll ring him up and tell him to get lost." She flung herself on the rug and sobbed her heart out. Mark was more philosophical, soon getting out maps and a railway timetable to argue that with a bit of luck he would be able to continue at his present school, making the fifty miles a day round trip by train and bus.

The parish itself had to be told, of course, and before long the dreaded goodbyes were on my lips. For nine years I had been part of a very close-knit community, privileged to share the joys and sorrows of many lives, but now the relationship was to be ended. Unlike most other folk who move, our departure had to have a particular finality about it, for this is one of the burdens a parish priest carries. Once he leaves a place, it is considered unprofessional for him to return. Of course, he can go back after a few years to preach for a special occasion or something of the sort, but that is about the limit. He is most certainly not expected to visit old friends or be seen walking about his old territory.

All this stems from the danger there would be of a priest interfering in his successor's work and strategy. Human nature being what it is, there would be some who would complain to the old incumbent of the antics of the new, for every clergyman makes his own special contribution to the life and work of a parish. In the Church of England, ministries are very personal, with every man bringing his own gifts and style, but this freedom can only exist when certain disciplines are observed, and one of them is a willingness to "let go" completely when the time comes. It has to be, "When you're gone, you're gone", if the system is to work at its best. The fact that this means severing links with friends who have been as close and dear as Walter, for instance, is the price to be paid. There was little sweetness in partings that felt close to bereavements, and it was with a leaden heart that I worked my way round the parish making my farewells.

These were specially difficult in the case of the old and infirm, with so many apparently facing a bleak future. With some I pretended things were other than they were. "When I'm round these parts, I'll pop in and say hello sometime." I knew it was not true, they knew the same, but at least it made it easier for me to walk out of their doors for the last time.

I said something of the sort to old Mrs. Gregory in Virgil Street. Sitting there in her wheelchair, with little mobility but much pain in her body, she smiled and played her part. "Yes, you do that," she said. It was one of the most poverty-stricken houses in the parish. A spread of newspaper served as a tablecloth, the curtains were dirty and cobwebby, and ashes galore littered the hearth. By the wheelchair, stood her middle-aged son, a grin on his face, his head moving up and down all the time like a yo-yo. Mentally handicapped, he was able to do little jobs about the house under her supervision, but obviously provided little real companionship for this very intelligent woman.

I had taken my leave and got to the door when she called me back. "Vicar," she said, "I want you to remember this. God is good." To make sure I had got the message she repeated it: "Always remember, God is good."

"Yes, sure," I replied, as I gave a final wave of the hand and let myself out of the door. What she had said sounded almost like blasphemy in my ears, so incongruous her words in that environment. I trudged on with the dismal business of saying goodbye to the housebound, feeling depressed. It was when I was on my way home that my thoughts returned to that poor house. I could only think that maybe there were factors in the situation not easily recognised. Mrs. Gregory was neither conventional nor sentimental. Maybe my face had betrayed my feelings, and she had wanted me to know that things were not as unbearable as they seemed. There was only one thing I could think of that would have done anything to alleviate her circumstances — and that would be difficult to express in words. Perhaps, "God is good" was as near as she could get to it. Brother Lawrence would probably have called it, "The Practice of the Presence of God."

Doing his daily chores in the monastery, he was able to write: "In the noise and clutter of my kitchen, while several persons are at the same time calling for different things, I possess God in as great tranquillity as if I were upon my knees at the Blessed Sacrament ... I turn the cake that is frying in the pan, and for love of Him, prostrate myself, and rise happier than a king."

Walter Hilton (died 1396), one of the earliest English spiritual writers, warned his readers, "not to tend God's head and neglect His feet". I was comforted with the thought that maybe old Mrs Gregory had found God's feet in her humble home. It was lovely to think that like the first Disciples, who had experienced the appearing and disappearing of Jesus after the Resurrection, and must have learned to look for Him day by day, she may also have developed the great spiritual gift of expectancy; like the poet says:

"So I am watching quietly every day,
Whenever the sun shines brightly, I rise and say,
'Surely it is the shining of His face',
And when a shadow falls across the room
Where I am working my appointed task,
I lift my head, and watch the door, and ask
If He is come?"

The move took place on a bitterly cold January day once more. Janet had tears in her eyes when the time came for us to walk out of the house for the last time. "Let's all turn and wave a last goodbye to the Vicarage," she suggested as we walked to the car parked in the road outside.

"Certainly not," said Joyce, "we've finished with goodbyes for the time being, there's no more looking back, just forwards now to the great time ahead. Mark my words, there will be happiness and contentment in store for us all. And for goodness sake, cheer up; anybody would think we were going to a funeral." I let out the clutch, pressed the accelerator, and we moved off towards our new home at Ashton Rectory.

It was a large, rambling Victorian house, isolated at the end of a long drive bordered on each side with high rhododendron bushes. It was Joyce who produced the nickname "Wuthering Heights", for obvious reasons, and it stuck. Set in extensive grounds, it had been a private residence until bought as a parsonage house in the early 1900s. C. P. Scott, famous editor of what was then the *Manchester Guardian* had at one time lived here, and was vaguely remembered for the fact that he rode the seven miles into Manchester each day on a push-bike.

If a house can look as though it should be haunted, this was it. But fortunately none of us was nervous in that respect, which was just as well, for we had not been living there long before odd things started to happen. Sometimes footsteps were heard along the landing when no-one was in that part of the house. Electric lights were switched on regularly in a rather mysterious way. We never fathomed these things in spite of tests and traps! But we did calm ourselves with the assurance that in such an old house, the plumbing and the wiring were probably faulty and unreliable, quite capable of causing noises and 'electrical happenings' beyond our understanding. The floorboards too creaked dreadfully, and what with the wind and draughts, loose slates and ill-fitting windows, it was easy to rationalise the odd things that came our way from time to time.

It was more difficult to rationalise the unusual things that happened with our bed clothes. For one thing, we often discovered that our bed had been 'unmade' when we went to get in it at the end of the day. Neat and tidy an hour before, it was not unusual once or twice a month to find it pulled apart with sheets and blankets strewn all over the place. We got used to grumbling about it as we made it again before taking our rest. Joyce dismissed the whole thing in her usual practical way: "If ghosts are responsible, it's a pity they haven't something better to do!" At first we had blamed the children, but when it happened when they were away, it was less easy to sustain the suspicion.

A more dramatic version of the 'psychic' bed-stripping happened several times when people were actually in the bed under 'attack', but on these occasions it was a different bed and a different bedroom, the one normally used for guests. At weekends, a friend of my daughter regularly stayed overnight. For courage and company in this rather creepy house they slept together in the guest room. Often they would wake feeling cold, to find the bed clothes pulled completely off them, and lying, not at the sides, but at the foot of the bed. Other visitors experienced the same kind of thing, and once when Joyce's sister and her husband stayed, they related how they had got involved in a tug-o'-war in the early hours as the clothes were pulled from them. They lost the contest and had to get out of bed to retrieve the blankets from the usual position. They came to breakfast with strained faces, vowing never to visit us again in that house, a promise they steadfastly kept!

In spite of all this, neither Joyce nor I ever came to believe in ghosts. It was best to be agnostic about some things, we agreed, though of course we had read about poltergeists and similar phenomena, often connected with the strange energies emanating from teenage children. We were aware too of the theories linking powerful past events with unusual happenings years later, but we felt all these things were of doubtful validity or importance, and so tended to ignore the unexplained events that sometimes occurred.

There was another reason, too, why this type of thing failed to alarm us. Largely unspoken, even taken for granted, was a basic belief in the love and wisdom of God. We could not for the life of us attribute to Him 'ghoulies and ghosties and things that go bump in the night'. The idea that the spirits of the dead were roaming our house at night, playing tricks on the living, was something we could not swallow, an affront to our common sense, and out of tune with what we knew of God's world. If this sounds arrogant, then it must be said in mitigation that we were prepared to admit "there are more things in heaven and earth than are dreamt of", but that was where we moved from God's wisdom to His protective love, and we were content to leave it at that.

However, oddly enough, there were folks in the ancient town of Ashton-under-Lyne, who were hoping I would be haunted, particularly in my early months there. They even wrote to tell me this. How dare I allow the graves of their forebears to be disturbed? they demanded. Several abusive phone calls assured me I would be punished "by the spirits" for the gross act of sacrilege I was permitting in the churchyard. A letter to a local newspaper described me as an "ecclesiastical vandal bent on desecration".

I did not relish either the description or the circumstances that gave rise to it. The last thing I wanted to happen was this, but Lancashire County Council had decided to build a new by-pass for the town that went right through the middle of the old churchyard which surrounded the ancient parish church. Two thousand 'bodies' had to be dug up and taken to the public cemetery a couple of miles away. The church had no option in the matter, for the land was acquired by the County Council with a compulsory purchase order. I managed to win a few concessions after some hard bargaining, the most important of which was the doubling of the distance between the new road and the church building. We were obviously concerned to keep the noise of traffic down to a minimum, but considering that the church possessed some of the most important medieval stained-glass in England, it was also important to reduce the danger that came from traffic vibration.

Eventually the dozen or so workmen with their bulldozers moved in to begin the grisly task of exhumation. They were employed by a London firm that specialised in this type of operation. It had been agreed that mechanical diggers would not be used to lift coffins and human remains though, of course, they were used for the preliminary work. A high wooden screen was erected on each side of the swathe that ran through the church grounds, and thus the work was carried on out of the public gaze. It needed to be done like that for it was as messy, smelly and distasteful as could be imagined.

The site manager was a former undertaker who had been born for this kind of thing. Tall, lean, with a cadaverous face, he had a lugubrious manner to match. Dressed in a shiny black suit with what had once been a white shirt, he would stand in the entrance of the wooden hut that served as his office, rubbing his long bony fingers together as he surveyed the scene of desolation that surrounded him. And with such relish too, that a thin, sickly smile was invariably present on his taut face. "Speedy by name, Speedy by nature," he had said when I met him for the first time, though I was soon to discover that no-one else would have dreamt of using a pun so grossly inappropriate. I got the impression he enjoyed the job so much that he was loath to see the kind of progress most of us longed for.

Two or three times a week I visited the site, partly out of curiosity, partly in an attempt to encourage greater headway. Each Thursday morning at 10.30 am I had a Communion Service in church, and I made it a practice to have a look at the churchyard first. On one particular occasion, I gave myself more than an hour for the inspection for I specially wanted to look at some of the gravestones that were being moved.

I climbed the two wooden steps leading to Mr. Speedy's office and stood on the small platform in front of the door. For once he was inside, and I saw he had one foot on the desk chair as he vigorously used a clothes brush to remove mud from his trouser turn-up. Catching sight of me, he put the brush down and joined me outside.

Standing side by side we looked at the sombre scene around us, one with distaste, the other pleasure. "It looks like a battlefield in the Great War," I said. "Trenches, mud, and even primitive tanks, to say nothing of the gallant soldiers." I pointed to the labourers busy with their spades.

"It's going quite well, guv," he volunteered in the words he always used, "but the heavy rain earlier this week has turned the place into a quagmire. My word, Rector, look at your shoes and your trouser bottoms; you'll only be able to brush it off when it's dry, so it's no good my offering the brush."

I became aware that my feet were wet and that I had gone over the shoe-tops. "I'm witchit, Mr. Speedy, witchit, but I don't suppose a Londoner knows what that means. Slutched up, too, and I'll bet that's a new word for you as well. But you can forget that for now because I really want to talk to you this morning about words of a different kind — the words on the gravestones." Mr. Speedy nodded invitingly, happier when dealing with his own speciality.

"You know, of course, that we have put a blob of red paint on the stones we hope to retain — about 250 of them. They'll be used for the new paths and other features in the landscaping. Your men do know that these have to be carefully preserved, don't they?"

"But of course, of course," Mr. Speedy replied, "you and your people must have worked very hard picking out the most interesting. I'm afraid the rest — hundreds of them — will have to be broken up. It's sad, but there's no other way."

"Presumably these are the ones being kept," I said, pointing to the thirty or forty piles of stones in the vicinity. It was like a miniature Stonehenge, with each columm containing half a dozen stones, laid flat on each other with a brick at the corners in between. Other stones were propped vertically against the sides of the columns. "You seem to have found a good way of stacking them," I remarked, "do you mind if we take a closer dekko?" He walked with me as I made my way towards them.

"I like this one, Rector," he said, as we came alongside the first pile. "Bit of humour here from the year 1840." Mr. Speedy began to read from the top horizontal stone:

"Here lies a Ringer beneath this cold clay
Who has rung many peals both serious and gay;
Through Grandsire and Trebles with ease he could
  range,
Till Death called the Bob and brought round his last
  change."

That was obviously his type of drollery; he was still chuckling as he pointed to one propped up by the side. "This is one of the oldest in the churchyard, isn't it? And who said everybody died young in the old days? John Leech here was 92 when he kicked the bucket in 1689." Again, Mr Speedy started to read:

"In Memory of John Leech, husband of Ann, and they had issue of 12 children, and in his time he was father of 12, grandfather of 75, great-grandfather of 92, and great-great-grandfather of 2, in all making 181."

"Very different from this one," I commented, as I spotted one of the many commemorating the deaths of several children. "Look, Robert Gregory died in 1819 aged 62; his wife Judith died nine years later, aged 73; but, poor things, they buried seven children, six of them babies, though their daughter was 24 when she died."

"Common enough that," said my companion, rubbing his hands together, but from habit, I thought, rather than pleasure. "No wonder this gentleman was kept busy." He had stopped in front of another stone in memory of one Isaac Miller, a Joiner, who had died in 1839. "Listen to this:" he then intoned, "In the Course of his life he made 5,443 Coffins." I made no comment, but I thought Isaac might have been a man after Mr Speedy's own heart.

We moved together round the various stacks. It was reassuring to see they had not been damaged in the move, in spite of their weight and age. "You will no doubt have noticed," said Mr Speedy, "that quite a few of the epitaphs are in the form of a message to the living — telling them to do something. Ah, here's an example:

"Mourn not for me, since life is past,
But look on me and pity take
On my dear children for my sake."

"There's an even better example of trying to speak from the grave here," he said as he disappeared round another group of stones to find the one he wanted to bring to my attention. Hidden from view, he had raised his voice to make sure I could hear: "This is in memory of Joseph Hardy, a miner," he called, "killed in the pit in 1807; his companion was John Andrew:

"Impelled by imprudent care,
Each other vainly daring strives
Through suffocating death-damp air
To fetch a pick, thus lost their lives.
Hence Miners all, this serious warning take,
And cautious care a constant rule to make."

153

"I'll have to be going," I told Mr. Speedy. "I have a Service in church in half an hour, but I am specially interested in one of the stones that I haven't spotted this morning. Of course, I know most of the inscriptions are hidden by the way the stones are stacked, so I am sure it will be here somewhere."

"Which are you referring to, Sir?" he asked, looking slightly worried.

"The one they say has something of a curse on it," I replied, "I think it might be of special historical interest."

Mr. Speedy's face went even more solemn than usual. "Will you come to my office, please," he invited. "I wanted a word with you on that score, anyway. I have something very important to say." He propelled me by the arm in the direction of the hut. Once inside he gained time and composure by clearing his throat, lighting a cigarette, and then slowly taking his chair behind the desk. He was looking nervous as he motioned me to sit in the wooden folding chair in front.

"Time for a confession, Rector," he began, "but first you must admit I am looking after the gravestones as carefully as possible — right?" I nodded an assent. "Pride myself I do," he continued, "on being an honourable man, and these people, long dead, paid good money to undertakers and stone-masons to rear these memorials. Being in the trade myself I'm aware of that. I want to preserve as many as possible and ..."

"Sorry to cut you short, Mr. Speedy but I am in a hurry. Forgive me, but what is it you want to say?"

He swallowed hard before replying. "To be perfectly honest," he said, "first thing this morning I've actually smashed one of the gravestones to pieces." He paused to let it sink in.

"I see, an accident presumably," I said, "well, these things do happen even to the best of us. I know some of them weigh a ton, and they are awkward to move. Did it slip out of the jaws of the lifting machine?"

"Oh no, nothing like that," he said quickly, "I'm saying

154

that I literally smashed it to pieces — with a sledgehammer — small pieces too — and I've already carted them away and thrown them into the infill for the new road."

"Really," I said in astonishment, "why on earth would you do a thing like that?"

"It was the one you were asking about — the one with the curse on it. I had no option. The men refused to start work this morning until I'd destroyed it." He picked up a sheet of paper from the desk. "Do you remember what it said, Rector?" He read the epitaph from the paper:

"Let no rude hand with spade prepare
To dig the dust interred here,
But let it rest on this its bed
Till rocks do rend and graves give up the dead."

Mr. Speedy's voice and manner seemed to indicate that everything was now satisfactorily explained. He looked extremely solemn and gloomy.

I did not know whether to be amused or angry. It seemed such a senseless thing to have done. "Why did it merit such drastic treatment?" I asked. "I must admit I did want specially to keep that one. I don't know why you interpreted those words as a curse. I'm genuinely surprised that a man of your experience should do a thing like that."

"It was the men themselves who were responsible" explained Mr. Speedy. "Since we lifted that stone a fortnight ago, we've had nothing but trouble. The very same day, a stone toppled on Reg and broke a bone in his foot. The next weekend, Alan had a car accident and finished up in hospital. Several of the men have had sickness and diarrhoea, and now we've been told that old Charlie, the night watchman, has had a stroke and won't work again. That was the last straw. They were waiting for me when I got to work this morning. 'Either that goes, or we do' they said, so I got out the hammer and whammed it. Couldn't risk the men downing tools at this stage; would have been difficult if not impossible to find replacements; not everybody can do this kind of work, you know.''

I saw his logic and got up to go. ''No good crying over spilt milk,'' I said, ''let's forget it.'' I did not bother to point out the illogicality of his action. It was not his gravestone the long-dead man had said should remain, but his dust — his bones. I held my peace for I had no desire to see bones being put back in the ground. The task in hand was to take them up, put them in little green plastic bags, and at the end of each day, take them to their new resting place in Hurst Cemetery.

I said goodbye and headed for the gate in the wooden fence that would put me just outside the church door. The congregation was beginning to arrive, but I had time to change my shoes before the appointed hour. I had started keeping spare socks and shoes in the Vestry since the commencement of the work. This was not the first time I was glad Joyce had persuaded me to do it.

It was not only my feet that had a different feel now. The grisly unpleasant scene outside was put aside, as the peace of the church building and the power of the liturgy took over. The light coming through the ancient windows bathed the church in gentle colours as we gathered round the Altar to break bread and pour the wine. A timeless thing to do, with the thin veil between our world and eternity pulled aside for a space, as we were transported in mind and spirit, to the time when Christ gave His body and shed His blood for our sake and our salvation. In this, as in all things, He knew so well the needs of ordinary people. And so He gave us this simple and effective way of taking into our lives His forgiveness and ''all other benefits of His passion''.

> Hail, sacred feast which Jesus makes,
> Rich banquet of His Flesh and Blood!
> Thrice happy he who here partakes
> That sacred stream, that heavenly food.

Soon I was standing at the door for a word with the congregation as they went out. As usual, Mrs. Duffy was the last to go. A round, jolly woman in her late sixties, she eked out her pension by cleaning some of the local offices. Known to everybody as "a good sort", she was good humoured and generous. As she came towards me, she opened the large leather shopping bag she always carried, and took out half a bar of chocolate.

"There you are, Rector," she beamed, "Cadbury's Milk; I know you like it. I bought the whole bar for you, but I got hungry on my way here — hope you don't mind."

I took it with a word of thanks and a smile. Whenever I was with her there was always a delightful feeling of anticipation as I wondered what was coming next, for she was capable of coming out with some very extraordinary things. Sometimes her "verbal gems" were deliberate, sometimes not. In the latter category were the malapropisms that flowed easily from her lips, particularly when dealing with medical matters. A short time before she had asked me to visit one of her neighbours in the same street.

"You must go, Rector," she urged, "old Mrs. Gradwell is having such trouble with her eyes; the doctor thinks it's a detached rectum."

I kept a straight face and promised to go. She was always a mine of information about people's ailments. She had immediately followed that one with, "Did you know Albert Jones has had his leg off? Poor fellow, they've taken it off right down to the foot," she added a dramatic wave of the hand to her own lower extremities. She was at her best when dealing with disease and death. Her voice would drop to a whisper if she considered the subject slightly indelicate, like the time she told me that her friend Gert would only be in hospital for a day or two; dropping her voice and making her lips work overtime, she hissed, "It's only bellicose veins, you know, bellicose veins." She left me open-mouthed in surprise one day when she confided, "When my husband died, he lost his voice." I felt there was no answer to that!

However, today was different. She was more theologically inclined. "Heard you ringing the bell for Mattins this morning at eight," she said, "I was cleaning the senior partner's office at the time." One of her "places" was the Solicitor's Office across the road. She continued, "The boss came in and asked me what the bell was for — he's not often there at that time of day. So I told him that you were going to say Morning Prayer and that the bell was to remind us all, wherever we were, to say a prayer too."

She paused for breath, ready to enjoy what was coming next. "The boss said to me, 'Does anybody ever go and join the Rector?'; Oh yes, I says, there's never less than four there — the Rector, the Father, the Son, and the Holy Ghost." She laughed loud and long. "Should have seen his face. But it's true, isn't it, absolutely true."

I refrained from answering for I did not want to get involved in a detailed theological discussion on the nature of the Blessed Trinity. I felt maybe she was emphasising the separateness at the expense of the unity, and that St. Athanasius would not have been very happy with her arithmetic! It was necessary to change the subject. "Nice to see you here Sunday night," was all I could think of.

It was a mistake. She then proceeded to give me a resumé of the sermon I had preached on that occasion. "Ee Rector, I did enjoy it. I'd never realised before what Jesus meant when He said we were to be ready to give to others a cup of cold water. Like you said, warm water would have been easy, for there it was in the urn, standing inside the house, having been drawn earlier in the day. But cold water — well that was a different matter. It meant going out in the hot sun to draw again from the well." When she paused for breath, I got a word in edgeways.

"Glad you listened so carefully," I said, hoping the play-back was now over. I started to move away in the direction of the Vestry, feeling she had been given sufficient time.

"See you soon, Mrs. Duffy."

She did not like leaving her tale half told. Raising her voice to follow me down the aisle, she said, "What you were saying, Rector, was that we have to put ourselves out to help one another; should be a costly thing — that right?"

I confirmed that that had been the message. By now I was five yards from her. I waved a goodbye and headed for the Vestry. I looked forward to getting home and having a coffee. I knew Joyce would be interested in the case of the sinister gravestone that had been made to disappear.

I had longer to wait for that than expected. For one thing, Bill Bardsley, the Verger, was waiting in the Vestry with a question that was troubling him as well as others in the parish. "I'm sorry to delay you, but folk keep coming in church and asking me about it. What have I to say? All these two thousand bodies being moved out of their graves. What will happen on Resurrection Morning when the souls come looking for their bodies, only to find they've gone? It worries some of us, you know. That's one reason why we don't like cremation."

He was looking very concerned as he ended his question with a quotation from the Creed: "'I believe ... in the Resurrection of the body; And the Life everlasting. Amen.' Have we stopped believing in that now?"

"No, we haven't stopped believing in that at all," I replied, "but the vast majority of Christians have never believed that the physical body would be put together after it had disintegrated to be reunited with the soul. From the very beginning, St. Paul made it clear that 'flesh and blood cannot inherit the Kingdom of God'. He said we are given instead, what he calls, 'a spiritual body'."

I started to take off my robes and put them in the cupboard. Bill sat on the large table that served as desk. "Bit daft, if you ask me," he said, "why talk about a body at all; wouldn't it be better if we were just taught that it's the soul that lives on — less confusing for everybody?"

I sat down in the desk chair, realising I was not going to be allowed to get away with a one-liner. "It's all to do with ideas of the after-life that were current in those early years of Christianity," I said. "In the Greek world, there was the belief that at death a person was absorbed into the Infinite — sort of swallowed up into something bigger, but losing individuality. And among some of the Jews, there was a curious notion that after death people's souls, looking a bit like sky-blue rugby balls, floated around hades in a shadowy existence. It was to counteract these ideas, that St. Paul and the others talked about a 'spiritual body'."

Bill pulled a face. "I'm going to have a difficult job explaining all that," he said.

"I'll tell you what," I replied, "just explain that having a spiritual body after death is a way of saying their personalities survive, that they will be recognisable, the same person. Like Jesus after the Resurrection: people knew Him, but He was obviously different, able to disappear, go through closed doors, and so on. However, the continuity was there, the nail prints in His hands and feet were one way of emphasising that."

"Right, I'll have a go," he promised.

"Stress the positive side if you can, Bill," I urged. "Our belief is that life after death is marvellous; sitting on a cloud playing a harp is rubbish; it will be more interesting, varied, exciting than anything we've known here. The Bible makes that clear. I can understand folk being afraid of dying — you know, how they actually pop off — but I can't understand why they should be afraid of death, knowing about God as we do. When we came into this world we were not unexpected and not unwelcome. Loving hands cared for us. I can't believe our Heavenly Father is less kind than our earthly mother, can you? Sorry, Bill, I'm starting to preach, it's an occupational hazard!" I got up to go as Bill pondered these things.

I had reached the gate outside when I saw Mrs. Duffy

hurrying back in my direction. I thought she would have been long gone by now. I quailed at the sight, but could do nothing other than stand and wait her arrival. She was breathless and flushed as she came up to me. ''Am I glad to see you,'' she began, ''I was worried in case you'd gone.''

The fact I wished devoutly I had disappeared from the scene was hidden from her as I forced a smile. Another few minutes would have been sufficient — if only I had not got involved in a theological discussion. ''What's the matter?'' I asked, ''you look all hot and bothered.''

''Locked out,'' she exclaimed in dismay. ''Been through this bag with a toothcomb for the key, but no luck, it's gone.'' She pushed the bag under my nose inviting a rummage, but I did not accept. I could see it was jam-packed with rubbish; I was surprised she could ever find anything in it. ''Whatever am I going to do?'' she moaned.

''Don't worry,'' I said reassuringly, ''there must be some way of getting into your house. Let's go and have a look. Like they say in films, 'we'll case the joint'. This will be a good way of finding out whether we would have made good burglars.''

Twice we walked round the house, testing the doors as well as the windows. On the ground floor everything was securely fastened. Then Mrs. Duffy spotted it; I had pretended not to see it; a small casement window in the gable-end had the top section pulled down an inch or two. ''Aren't we lucky,'' beamed the good lady, ''I know where we can get a ladder; the man next door has one in his yard. He's at work, but he won't mind if you borrow it. It's like I always say, 'Where there's a will, there's a way'. Come on, I'll show you.''

I followed her with a bogus enthusiasm that a child of three would have seen through. I was scared stiff, for although I could climb a ladder without too many qualms, the thought of getting off it anywhere other than the bottom brought me out in a cold sweat.

The ladder was heavy and difficult to handle. I had seen

the experts put a shoulder through a rung and walk with it upright. I tried to do the same. There was much swaying and weaving, with every window in range at risk. Finally, however, it stood in approximately the right place. I stood holding on to it for support, for I was shaking slightly from the exertion and from sheer terror.

Mrs. Duffy must have sensed I needed further encouragement. "Ee Rector," she said, "this is that cup of cold water you were talking about on Sunday night; you really are putting yourself out for me, aren't you?" I tried to smile as I wiped my hands on a handkerchief — I did not want my grip to be impaired in the slightest degree. With a last fond look at the ground, I put a foot on the first rung and started to go up.

The ladder was too long, and hence the gap between me and the open window seemed enormous. Hanging on like grim death, I took a breather. I was thinking what a classic case this was of being hoist with my own petard. I did not even have the satisfaction of feeling virtuous, and for some reason T. S. Eliot's words came into my mind: "The fourth temptation is the greatest treason, to do the right thing for the wrong reason". I had no doubt whatsoever that I was facing this hazard for the wrong reason. Partly I had been bullied into it, partly I felt my job required me to play the role of Good Samaritan now and again.

The pause must have been long enough for Mrs. Duffy to suspect I might be chickening out; she offered further Biblical encouragement: "Great shall be your reward in heaven". Added to my cowardice, that might just have been enough to enable me to swallow my pride and literally climb down, but by this time a few of Mrs. Duffy's cronies who lived in the street had assembled around her, and I could not face such public humiliation. I put out a hand to the bottom section of the window and managed to push it up. More by accident than design, I had got the ladder in the right position to one side, and now I simply lunged forward, head first through the opening. Half in, half out, I realised there was a drop

of six or seven feet to the bedroom floor. Somehow, I managed to drag my legs inside, hanging on to the window ledge as I turned my body round, before finally lowering myself to the floor.

Alas, only one foot was fortunate enough to land on the lino. The other went straight into Mrs. Duffy's china chamber-pot, which could not have been in a more strategic position had she positioned it for the arrival of an intruder. And, like her large leather shopping bag, the room was a mixed-up jumble with bed unmade, pot unemptied. With a grimace of distaste, I shook my shoe over the pot like a dog shakes itself after a swim. Then, when convinced that no further extraction was possible, I pushed the pot under the bed to avoid embarrassment — mine, rather than hers, I suspected. The next move was to negotiate the stairs, with one foot feeling distinctly peculiar, before turning the knob on the Yale lock and opening the door.

Mrs. Duffy and her neighbours rushed in full of congratulations. The chief beneficiary led them in their praises of the heroic feat they had witnessed. She searched for superlative after superlative to express her admiration. And, like the ripples in a pond when a stone has been thrown in, the extent of her adulation went wider and wider, starting with the Rector but quickly moving to the parish, the Diocese, the Church of England, and finally the Anglican Communion throughout the world. Her paean of acclaim reached its climax with a question she addressed to one Ada Thistlethwaite, whom I knew to be a pillar of the local chapel. "Ada," she asked, "now be honest, you wouldn't get the Methodist Minister climbing through your bedroom window, would you?"

With a sad shake of the head, Ada indicated she thought this highly unlikely. My admiration and respect for the minister, already very high, went up three more notches in as many seconds!

Firmly resisting an invitation to celebrate the occasion with a glass of Irish whiskey, I made my escape, and started to squelch my way home. Mrs. Duffy, not easily deterred, followed me half way down the street still pressing liquid refreshment of one kind or another. "Are you sure you won't wet your whistle," she called in a last desperate invitation. I waved without looking back, feeling I had wet enough for one morning, for to be witchit twice within a couple of hours was too much of a good thing. On arrival at the Rectory, I put my wet sock in the dustbin by the back door, swilled the foot itself under a tap in an outbuilding, and still shaking it with a recently acquired skill, made my way inside for a long-delayed cup of coffee.

Joyce was not amused. "You must be mad to take such risks," she asserted, "there's nothing noble about stupidity, and mark my words, one of these days you'll come to grief doing things like that." (A few years later I remembered her words rather ruefully as I lay in a hospital bed with a broken spine after a fall from a ladder.) She continued to lay down the law, concluding with yet another warning: "And if I were you, I would ration 'Good Samaritan' sermons, or you might get yourself into more hot water." She quickly made an amendment: "Maybe I should have said 'tepid' water, more accurate don't you think?" Her laugh indicated she was getting over the alarm that had produced the anger.

With the reprimand out of the way, I was able to recount the tale of the broken gravestone. "I wouldn't let it bother you," advised Joyce, "I don't think it was all that important, do you?"

"I think it was," I said, "and I'll tell you why. It might just have been the only bit of evidence we've got that Ashton was plagued with the awful business of body-snatching. Why else would anybody compose an epitaph like that — about rude hands with spade disturbing the grave? It's about the right period — first half of the nineteenth century, and we do know that about that time bodies were dug up in this area and sold to medical students."

We were having coffee in the study. I took down a slim volume from the bookshelves. "This is a short history of Mottram church," I said, "only three or four miles away, and I want you to listen to this epitaph from about the same period." I found the place and started to read the words composed by the anguished parents of a fourteen year old boy:

"Though once beneath the ground his corpse was
laid,
  For use of surgeons it was thence convey'd.
Vain was the scheme to hide the impious theft;
  The body taken, shroud and coffin left.
Ye wretches who pursue this barb'rous trade,
  Your carcases in turn may be convey'd
Like his, to some unfeeling surgeon's room;
  Nor can they justly meet a better doom."

I put the book down on the desk. "Like you say, no good bothering about it now, what's done is done." I held up my bare foot: "Need to put some other socks on: are you going to be kind and get me a pair?"

There was no answer from Joyce as she moved quickly into the hall to answer the 'phone. I was still sitting there minus a sock when she returned a few minutes later. To deliver her message with maximum effect she raised her eyebrows: "Do you think it's got around that you've started climbing into ladies' bedrooms in the parish," she asked sweetly, "for why else would a newspaper be so anxious to speak to you? Oh by the way, it's not the *Ashton Reporter*, it's *The News of the World*. Shall I tell them you are not available at the moment?"

"A tempting offer," I replied, "but one I can't accept." With a bare foot I hobbled towards the 'phone. Over my shoulder I admitted, "I'm not surprised curiosity killed the cat — it's a powerful motivating force."

CHAPTER EIGHT

"Genius does what it must, and Talent does what it can." (Owen Meredith, 1831-1891)

I came in from the early Communion Service to find that Joyce had already been out for a copy of *The News of the World*. It was propped up ready for me on the breakfast table. She said she had felt embarrassed asking for it. "The bloke in the shop gave me a very funny look."

"You should have told him you read it for the Sport, that's what everybody else says," I joked. "But is there anything in it? — about us, I mean, of course."

"Don't think so: I've flipped through it a couple of times, but you'd better make sure."

"Let's hope we can keep it that way, otherwise the balloon really will go up. It will be a nightmare. I'll probably be tarred and feathered, to say the least."

"What a lovely thought," said Joyce with an impish grin, "I've always wanted to see somebody tarred and feathered. If it's a public ceremony bags a front seat."

"I'm going down to the churchyard in the morning to see these two men, and then tomorrow night there's a meeting here of the Standing Committee. So say your prayers."

"The love of money is the root of all evil," quoted Joyce.

"You can say that again. I know it's not a fortune, but the *News of the World* has agreed to pay them £500 apiece for their story. Some folk would sell their souls for that kind of money. Well, they are not going to spoil my day: I'm forgetting about it until tomorrow." A promise only broken when I went to bed.

I was glad when morning came, and after Mattins and breakfast, I hurried to meet Mr. Speedy in his office. He

167

joined me as usual on the platform as I surveyed the scene. It was obvious the job was nearing completion for although it still looked a mess, the rows of graves to be exhumed were now confined to a small section at the far end of the churchyard.

"There'll be very little left in those graves over there," he said pointing a finger in the general direction. "In fact, many of them seem completely empty. The soil is sandy and it drains well; after a hundred years there's just nothing left; unusual even to find a single bone. Very different story, of course, in the other parts where there is clay and a lot of retained water. But I've no need to tell you that, you've seen it for yourself, haven't you?"

I nodded in agreement. Several times I had been present when the wet clayey conditions had resulted in a near-perfect coffin being brought up. And, even more surprising, with what appeared to be a near-perfect body inside. It was an odd feeling to look at a face that had been dead for nearly two hundred years. The sickening smell at such a time did not encourage me to linger. I knew the workmen were reasonably well paid, and as I saw them plunge their gloved hands into the box and lift out remains which seemed to disintegrate while they held them, I did not begrudge them a penny of their money. A bonfire was kept burning to dispose of the rotting coffin timbers.

Mr. Speedy had the kettle boiling ready for coffee. While he was making it I got down to business. "Now let me get this straight," I began, "two of your men have been in touch with the *News of the World* alleging serious misconduct in the way this whole business has been carried out. Is that right?"

"Quite right, Rector, quite right. I don't mean right in the sense that there's truth in what they say, but right in the sense that that is what they are saying. They've made it up — it's pure fabrication. I'd like to wring their necks. They're after the money, as you can guess. They even had the reporter here yesterday when I was away; had a photographer with him too;

they are signing what they call their 'true stories' at lunchtime today, in the Stamford Arms, I believe."

"Correct me if I'm wrong," I said, "but the sub-editor who talked to me on the phone said there were three areas that gave cause for alarm. He was full of righteous indignation, of course, as you would expect. He told me the first terrible thing was that all the valuables — rings, brooches, necklaces, etcetera, that were found on the dead, have been stolen, either by the men doing the work or by the church. Ever heard such rubbish? You know as well as I that we have made sure every single item of value has been reinterred with the remains on which it was found. But I'm afraid that will not stop the headline — I can see it now: 'Robbing the Dead' it will say."

"Then there's the business of dishonouring the dead?" groaned this former undertaker. "Among other things, these two rascals say it's been common practice to use a row of skulls on a shelf in the workmen's hut for dart practice every lunchtime. Again it's bilge, absolute bilge, but I'm told they staged a photograph of this yesterday, all ready for next week's paper. That really will put the cat among the pigeons?"

"The locals will be furious if they believe their forebears have been dishonoured in this way," I said. "They'll be ready to lynch both of us if they see that picture. Now the third thing is about this business with Professor Hardwicke, isn't it?"

"Yes," he said looking rather embarrassed. I knew he had disapproved of what I had done in this respect. "It was you Rector who gave permission for the medical research programme, wasn't it?"

I had to admit it was. The Professor and his team from the school of dentistry at Manchester University had been very anxious to take advantage of a unique opportunity to examine the teeth of folk who had lived in the eighteenth and nineteenth centuries. Apparently, this was the period that saw the introduction of refined sugar into the common diet, and hence here was an opportunity to chart its effect.

Mr. Speedy made the point I knew still rankled with him. "I seem to remember, Rector, that both the Home Office and the Diocesan Bishop refused permission for any medical involvement in the exhumations. It was you that allowed it to happen, wasn't it?"

He was rubbing it in, but he was quite right. Home Office and Bishop had said they did not have the authority to grant permission. One passed the buck to the other. It looked like a stalemate. So I had written a letter giving permission. It was probably not worth the paper it was written on, but it did the trick and got the show on the road. And it had proved worthwhile. The Professor assured me the findings were significant enough to find their way into some of the text books of the future. He and his team were delighted and, among other things, two or three new Ph D's had emerged.

"I only hope," said Mr. Speedy in his most doleful tones, "that the third headline isn't about you and the way you allowed medical experiments on the dead."

"That's rubbish," I snapped, "there were no experiments, just photographs of teeth and detailed examinations. All done carefully and with reverence; quickly too, for every set of remains was reinterred within twenty-four hours. I feel sure the dead would have approved of their remains being made useful for the living." A shake of the head told me I had not convinced my companion.

The summary of events was concluded just in time, for a knock at the door announced the arrival of the two protagonists. This was the first time I had seen them face to face. A big man and a little man, both wearing blue boiler-suits, and the little moustache under the nose of the big one, as well as their general physical appearance, prompted thoughts of Laurel and Hardy.

They were not in the least abashed by the encounter, rather aggressive in fact. "No good trying to talk us out of it," said Frank, the big one, "what we've said is the truth, the whole truth, and nothing but the truth. Right Eddie?" His diminutive partner said, "Aye, and it's only right that people should know what's been going on here."

They both puffed on their cigarettes defiantly. "Well now you know," said the big one, "is there anything else you want? 'Cause we're not going to waste any more time here."

"Don't you realise," I began, "that you're going to cause a lot of bother in this town with these wild allegations. And a lot of folk are going to be very upset at what they think has happened to their long-dead relatives. Have you no remorse? Will you do anything for money? I don't know how you'll be able to sleep at nights."

"We'll sleep very well, thank you," said Eddie, "especially with a couple of pints inside us. Come on Frank." They headed for the door still laughing. "So long mate," said one of them as they disappeared down the steps.

"Charming fellas," observed Mr. Speedy with heavy sarcasm.

"I'd like to bang their heads together," I said. "Mind if I use your phone?" I spoke to Leslie, the church treasurer, asking him to put on his other hat, for he was also a solicitor.

171

I briefly reported on my encounter with Eddie and Frank, and reminded him of our meeting at the Rectory later that day.

"Yes, of course, I'll be there," he said. "Oh and by the way, do you mind if we have the meeting in your dining-room?"

It struck me this was an odd request, but I said I did not mind, though I was still curious about it some hours later when he and the others arrived for our consultation. In a house of large rooms, the dining-room was the largest. Impressive too, with a splendid fire-place at the far end complete with a carved oak mantel-piece, and a grate below that could swallow a bucket of coal at a time. Down one side of the room were two bay windows overlooking the lawns. The oak parquet floor could be seen between and around the two large red carpets that brought a touch of colour to an otherwise sombre setting.

Leslie was the first to speak. Again he surprised me. "I think we need to move the furniture a bit, if you don't mind." He took the lead by getting hold of one end of the refectory table that stood in the middle of the room. "Can we have this broadside on in front of the fireplace, please?" I helped him put it where he wanted it. "Now the chairs, if you don't mind," he said, "one at each end, and the other four along the side of the table with their backs to the fire. I want this to look like a tribunal, even a court. Do you mind somebody pushing the round table in the bay further in? The room must look as large as possible." It was not difficult to achieve the desired effect in a room that sometimes accommodated up to forty or fifty people for a coffee evening.

"Will you please sit at the table now," Leslie invited, and the six of us complied. I found myself in what was obviously the chairman's position. "Haven't much time for explanations," Leslie said, "but I want you all to sit there looking very solemn. The two rascals behind our problem are due here in a few minutes, and we are going to interview them. Please leave the talking to me."

"How on earth did you manage to persuade them to come?" I enquired. "This morning they told me very definitely the talking was over — in fact, they were rude about it."

"Saw them in the pub at lunchtime, said I wanted very much to have a word with them this evening. As you can guess I got a bad reception — not only were they not interested, they were positively hostile. That is until I emphasised that I was the church treasurer. With a nod and a wink, I told them I had important matters to put before them for their careful consideration. They would hear something to their advantage, I said. I could see their greedy minds working. They actually think we are going to make them a counter offer in excess of the one from the *News of the World*. That's why they're coming. In fact, they've this minute arrived, I think, for if I'm not mistaken that was the doorbell."

Joyce tapped on the door and led them in. As she closed the door behind her, Leslie took over. "Stand here, please?" he said severely, indicating a position in front of the table. "There is an ash-tray on the sideboard on your left: cigarettes out, if you don't mind."

Surprisingly they went meekly to the side and stubbed them out. They needed no further instruction to resume their place in front of the table. They were both trying to look nonchalant and in control, but I sensed they were a bit over-awed by the scene. It was the big one who spoke. "Now then, what have you in mind? We've been good enough to come, so get on with it. Don't start appealing to our better nature or anything like that. You know what it is we're interested in; talk turkey, and cut the cackle."

All our eyes were on Leslie. He occupied one of the side chairs. Now he stood and opened the suitcase he had placed on the table in front of him. Three or four large legal tomes were removed and put on the table. Slowly, deliberately, and in silence, Leslie opened each one at a particular page indicated by a leather bookmark; they now covered most of the table. This completed, he addressed the two men.

"Thank you for coming, gentlemen," he began, "this is what we have in mind." He lifted the lid of the suitcase again, taking out two official-looking documents, blue foolscap with red wax seals at the bottom of each. With one in each hand, he turned them towards the two so that they saw them clearly. Bringing them back to a normal reading position he spoke again.

"These two depositions will shortly be signed by the members of this executive committee. There is one in respect of each of you. We want to be absolutely fair, and before signing and executing them, felt you should be aware of their contents. The consequences of what we are about to do will be so serious that in all conscience we felt it our Christian duty to acquaint you fully with our intentions. Do you understand?"

Frank and Eddie shuffled their feet, slightly uncomfortable. Still defiant, the answer came from Eddie: "Understand what? Too many big words there for me. What ya trying to do — blind us wi' science?" They looked at each other for support and grinned, keen to show they were not easily cowed. "How much is it worth if we keep our mouths shut? Stop messing about — put your cards on the table." This came from Frank emboldened by Eddie's cockiness.

Leslie stared at them in silence for ten seconds before speaking again. "You do not seem to understand. But listen carefully to what is contained in these documents." In his best court-room voice he began to read from one of them. "We the undersigned, citizens of the Borough of Tameside in the Metropolitan County of Greater Manchester, hereby notify and inform the Chief Constable of the said County, that Frank Collier, aged 47, residing for the time being at The Royal Oak, Old Street, Ashton-under-Lyne, has, of his own will, freely and voluntarily admitted complicity in a series of acts contrary to the common law of England. These are scheduled as follows: Item one: the aforesaid Frank Collier did unlawfully commit a grave act of sacrilege, in that he participated in the desecration of human remains. These had been lawfully exhumed under Home Office regulations, and were subjected to gross abuse in that Frank Collier, together with others, played darts with human skulls before they were reinterred in consecrated ground in the public cemetery at Hurst. He has in a signed statement to a national newspaper admitted this felony."

Leslie paused and raised his eyes from the document. In a pleasant voice he asked, "Now that is correct, isn't it? You have quite openly admitted the felony. No argument about that I take it?" He turned and faced Eddie.

"This other document, as you will have guessed, is exactly the same, except that your name is on it. And you are staying for the present at the same pub, aren't you? You have also admitted the felony. I'll go on now and read the second item."

"Hang on a minute," interrupted Frank, "what's it all mean? What's a 'felony'?"

Leslie's voice had lost none of its sweetness. "Felony? Oh it simply means a serious crime. The name of it, by the way, is sacrilege." He began straight away to read the second item. "Furthermore, the above mentioned Frank Collier has also admitted being party to the theft of gold rings and other valuable artefacts taken from the coffins and off the human remains exhumed lawfully in accordance with ..." He stopped and put the documents down on the table. "Do I need to go on? We are just telling the Chief Constable of this second felony — you know, this second serious crime against the laws of England: not sure whether this will be sacrilege again or theft. You can have no objections, surely; after all, it's all going to be printed in the paper."

A strange hush descended on the proceedings. The two looked at each other with dismay. Eddie took out a handkerchief and mopped his brow. There was a final attempt at cockiness from Frank. "Do what you like, makes no difference to us. You should have made sure these things didn't happen."

"That's not a crime," answered Leslie, "but what you admit to is. In a way, I do admire your honesty, if nothing else. You have certainly made a clean breast of it all. Not often that men make the job of the police so easy. The Chief Constable will no doubt just forward our statement to the Director of Public Prosecutions. Maybe the judge will be lenient in view of your confessions. You may only get eighteen months or two years. You could plead mitigation, and say you were carried along with the others who were doing these things. I expect they'll be arrested too in due time. If I can give you a word of advice, I think that when you come out of gaol, you should disappear, perhaps abroad, for you're not going to be very popular with your mates, are you?"

It was great drama. Those of us round the table hardly dared to breathe; we kept our eyes down. Finally, Frank spoke, addressing me, and with a very different tone, almost whining now: "Rector, you've come into the churchyard many a time since the job started. You know all this is rubbish. You'll tell the police nothing like these things ever happened, won't you?"

Leslie's eyes flashed a warning to me to speak with care and not to let them off the hook. "Sorry," I said, "but how can I do that when you've made a signed statement to the press admitting these things? I'll do what I can for your wives and families while you are inside, of course."

"But it was mainly a joke, wasn't it Eddie?" said Frank. "We made it up for a bit of fun, and to earn ourselves an extra bob or two. No harm in that, not a crime, say what you like." It was easy to see the fire had gone out of him.

Leslie rounded it all off. "If the newspaper prints that article, these documents I have prepared will definitely go to the police. I've told you what will happen after that. You really will be in big, big trouble. I advise you to get in touch with the *News of the World* at once."

"Your damned idea," grumbled Eddie to Frank, giving him as black a look as I had seen for a long time. He was clearly shaken, his face had gone white. Frank was still trying to bluster it out, spluttering "They can't do anything, can't do anything. All we have to do is ring up that reporter and tell him we've changed our minds, that's all, that's all. No need to panic."

"There's a phone in the study," said Leslie. "Come this way. I only hope for your sake you're in time." The two rushed out without a word.

It was getting on for half-an-hour before Leslie came back. He was alone. "I think it will be OK," he said, "but the northern editor wouldn't make any promises. Very annoyed with those two, as you can imagine, didn't half tear them off a strip. They told him there wasn't a word of truth in what they had said, and they got an earful in return, I can tell you. They looked very woebegone when Joyce took them to the front door; arguing like mad they were, blaming each other as they went out. Don't suppose we'll ever see them again for they have been laid off by the London firm. In fact, there are only a few men left working in the churchyard now that the job is practically finished."

At this stage, Joyce entered with the tea trolley laden with sandwiches and cakes. There was no sign of the teapot. "Thought this would be more appropriate tonight," she said triumphantly as she fished out a bottle of sherry from the sideboard. "Pity it's not champagne, but it's the thought that counts." She filled our glasses and a churchwarden proposed a toast: "To the unearthing of all grave felonies" he said solemnly.

A few days later, I had the satisfaction of reporting a successful outcome to the Archdeacon. I had kept him in touch with events in case of scandal, and he told me how relieved he was at the way things had ended. We were discussing the affair at the annual Rural Deans' Meeting at the Diocesan Conference Centre. He steered me into a corner during the lunch period. I assumed this was to hear of the affair in more detail, but I was wrong.

"Tell me," he said, "how are things with you personally these days — from the family point of view, I mean? How's Mark and Janet, and what are they doing at the present? And Joyce, of course: she all right?"

I gave him a resumé of the domestic scene. He took out an envelope and made notes on the back. "Mark reading Law at Durham; Janet in the sixth form; Joyce recovering after a bad bout of rheumatoid arthritis. Could you give me the ages of the children?" he asked, and they went on the envelope too. "Remind me of your hobbies," he said, and further notes were made.

When pen and envelope went back into his pocket I asked the obvious question. "What's all this about? Is it the KGB, the CIA, or MI5 that are on my tail? Come on, there was nothing very subtle about that interrogation, what's going on?"

He looked uncomfortable. "To tell you the truth," he said, "I'm not supposed to do that." His voice dropped to a whisper and he looked round to make sure no-one could hear. "It's just that we've had a letter from Saumarez Smith asking about you, and I wanted as much information as possible before replying."

I was not absolutely sure who Saumarez Smith was and the puzzlement must have shown on my face.

"He's the Archbishops' Secretary for Appointments?" explained the Archdeacon, "works with his opposite number at 10 Downing Street to produce names of suitable candidates for Bishoprics and other top jobs. They consult with the Archbishops and the Prime Minister when there is a vacancy, and finally the PM takes two names to the Queen, so that in theory she makes the choice, though it is said she invariably puts a tick and her initials alongside the first name. Then that's it."

When the Archdeacon spotted the surprise and alarm in my eyes he obviously regretted having said so much; he began to back-pedal as fast as he could. "It probably means nothing, nothing at all. We've had these enquiries before and nothing has come of them. Don't get excited, just forget it. And please, not a word to anyone, or it will be 'bell, book and candle' for me"

I felt slightly better. A routine enquiry, well, that did not sound too threatening. I drove home in an uneasy frame of mind, a quarter pleased, three-quarters apprehensive. Once home, Joyce worked her usual alchemy to bring peace. "You needn't worry," she said mischievously, "I'm sure the Church of England isn't that short of Bishops."

"Thanks a million," I replied, "with friends like you, who needs enemies!" But her words did have a certain ring of truth about them, and as the days and weeks slipped by, the incident receded comfortably to the back of my mind.

I would have been less tranquil had I known this was but the calm before the storm. Already cross currents were gaining momentum and troubled waters lay ahead. The fact is, I was not the only one who did not particularly want me to become a Bishop. Those most closely involved in London were putting up a stiff resistance to the idea, and rightly so I believe, for they were making the point that a Bishop should have talents that would enrich the whole Church rather than those that might just meet the needs of a particular Diocese.

I discovered later the details of the argument. It all stemmed from my old friend Victor Whitsey, recently appointed Bishop of Chester. I had been his immediate successor in two jobs — as Curate in Chorley, and nine years later, as Vicar of St Thomas, Halliwell. The Suffragan See of Birkenhead in his new Diocese was vacant, and it was customary for the Diocesan Bishop to have a major say in such an appointment. He had been sent a copy of the highly confidential 'Lambeth List', and had been asked to cast his eye over the field. In a covering letter, the Archbishops' Secretary explained the purpose of the 'List'. "This is my main tool," he said, "it contains about 300 names of men considered by their Diocesans to be potential Bishops, Deans, Provosts, or Archdeacons."

Victor was delighted to find my name on it, put there apparently the year before by Patrick, Bishop of Manchester. Since this supported his own inclination, he proceeded to forward my name for the vacant Bishopric, with the old principle about the 'devil you know' playing its part, no doubt, in his decision.

There was an immediate reaction from the centre. "Discount Ronald Brown of Ashton-under-Lyne," came the message, "for the fact that he was your own successor at St. Thomas', Halliwell would attract a good deal of criticism." The same letter went on to recommend most strongly the appointment of any one of seven priests, all of whom would bring special qualities to a task for which they were eminently suitable. Looking at the list some months later, when I had in fact taken up the appointment, I had to admit any one of them would have been splendid. There was a Professor of Theology at a British University; Residentiary Canons at three of our great Cathedrals; two parish priests who were lively members of General Synod; and one man, then a parish priest, but previously holding a senior position in one of the main theological colleges.

It was not modesty, but realism, that made me doubt the wisdom of Victor's choice, but nevertheless, I had the grace to rejoice in the unexpected and undeserved thing that had befallen me. Victor had argued with power and conviction that I was his first and only choice, and, supported by my own Bishop of Manchester, he had eventually won the day. He had answered in great detail the counter-arguments that came from London, namely that I was too much like him; secondly, that I was the wrong churchmanship; thirdly, that I was too young for the job; and finally, that if appointed, I could be a Suffragan Bishop for nearly twenty years, and would end up either bored, lazy, or sour, or all three! The letters went back and forth, but eventually even the Archbishop of York gave in, and Victor had his way.

I can honestly say that I would have been only too happy

to withdraw from the contest at any stage, and I sent a message to that effect, via my own Bishop, to the Archbishop of York. I assured him that if he felt unable to sign the Petition to Her Majesty the Queen, I would feel joy rather than pain. When I heard on the grapevine that he was hesitating, my hopes soared, and I thought how marvellous it would be to have been considered for a Bishopric without ever having to do the job, but then came the news that he had simply been away from Bishopthorpe for a few days and that, in fact, all was now completed. A few days later, I received a letter from the Prime Minister telling me that in the Queen's absence abroad, the Counsellors of State, on her behalf, "have been graciously pleased to approve that you be appointed Bishop Suffragan of Birkenhead ... I should like to send you my best wishes on your appointment to this important office. Yours sincerely, Edward Heath."

With the official announcement from 10 Downing Street, loads of letters, of course, began to arrive. One from a northern Suffragan contained a single word — "Commiserations."! Nearly all of them were kind and helpful, and I did not in the least mind the one or two that pointed out that once again the old maxim had been well illustrated, namely, it's not what you know, but who you know, that really counts. I could disagree neither with the maxim in general, nor with its particular application on this occasion. When I showed Victor one of these letters, he modified the proposition somewhat by saying the third factor that plays its part is what the person who knows you thinks of you! I valued his kind reassurance. And on the positive side, one of the most heartening things was that I would from now on be working closely with a man whom I did know very well indeed.

Victor Whitsey, the thirty-eighth Bishop of Chester, was a remarkable man by any standards, and a most unusual Bishop. He had quite a powerful physical presence, though at five foot ten or eleven he was not all that tall. It was probably his broad shoulders and thick-set arms that did it, and he had large hands: "Like shovels," he would say, holding them up for inspection.

In a sense, they typified the man. They were strong and tough, and he could use them with force and vigour as he used a spade to dig his garden, or swing an axe to produce logs for the fire. Yet these same hands could be used in a much more delicate way. He was a first-class joiner and could make a dove-tail with the best of them, and when his tools were laid aside, he could put his hand on a shoulder in sympathy and support, or enclose a smaller hand with tenderness in a sick-room or hospital ward.

This same contrast was evident in his life and character. One minute his hands would be used to thump a table as he laid down the law, the next they would be in his pocket as he pulled out a banknote to give to the very person he was shouting at. "I've told you bluntly lad why I think you've been a bee eff; now get yourself home, and take your wife out for a meal tonight, on me."

He had a deep, fruity voice that could quickly grow in volume for he had a short fuse, and the quickest way to arouse his anger was to bring him into a situation where he felt some injustice was being perpetrated, particularly if children were involved. He would raise his voice in anger at churchwardens who were bullying a weak vicar, or vice versa; get very het up and threaten a Diocesan committee if he felt it was not doing all it could for the welfare of the clergy, or if he suspected it was getting too powerful, or even if it greatly diverged from his own viewpoint for he was not a convinced believer in democracy. He was always ready to endorse the principle that "a camel is a horse designed by a committe", and made no secret of the fact that he much preferred an older and more Biblical style of leadership that came from individuals rather than groups.

He did not miss much of what went on in the Diocese for he had a sharp mind, and he expressed himself well too, particularly on paper, using his rare gift with words. It was not for nothing that he was a life-long fan of the great Dr. Johnson, and that he loved to read Hooker, Macaulay, and Winston Churchill. His frequent letters to *The Times* were welcomed not only by the editor, but by people all over the country, ranging as they did over all kinds of subjects, frivolous and serious, from the "fringe benefits" of a kingfisher that had taken up residence on the side of the goldfish pond in his garden in Chester, to suggestions on how to settle the miners' strike. There were more than fifty of them in all, and not infrequently they caused annoyance, even consternation, to members of the "establishment", and finger-wagging rebukes from his ecclesiastical superiors were not unknown!

It was easy to see why he had had such a meteoric rise to high rank in the Army during the War, going from Sergeant-Major to Lieutenant-Colonel in three short years. He was a man's man, enjoying a pint of beer and a hearty laugh, smoking his pipe with noticeable relish, and generally approving of the world around him. He was "earthy" in the best sense, believing he had impeccable New Testament precedence for walking firmly and confidently through a world which God had made and declared to be "good". His leadership was clear and decisive, sometimes right, sometimes wrong, but never muddled. It was, of course, a weakness as well as a strength that he tended to see things in black and white, but at any rate his focus was sharp and he knew where he wanted to go. His critics would have said this was normally "backwards", for he had a great regard for traditional things such as the Prayer Book, the King James' Bible, and the customary role of a priest in his parish. And it is true that he could at times be scathing about some of the modern alternatives, judging them banal and superficial, deeply troubled at the prospect of the Church being foolish enough to jettison things of tested worth and value for things less able to meet the real and deepest needs of ordinary people.

Victor had great pastoral gifts and a genuine care for people, particularly the clergy and their families in his Diocese. Most Monday mornings, clad in purple cassock and puffing his pipe, he would set out from Chester to visit where the Spirit led him, gradually over the years getting into most of the parsonage houses. "Just called to see that you're all right, lad," he would say, "any chance of a cup of tea?" He always returned with half a dozen things written on the back of an envelope that would remind him of how he could help this family or that. A cheque would go off to one; a telephone call to help a vicar's child get into a particular school would be made; and a hand-written letter of encouragement to another would catch the evening post. Careful notes and records were kept of all his visits, these casual ones as well as the more formal, for there was nothing slipshod or sporadic about his pastoral administration. He believed strongly in being available, and interviews were granted at short notice and on a prodigious scale, with more than 1,500 individuals being seen by him in his study over a period of twelve months — the only time a count of this kind was made. In addition, the official episcopal diary ensured that every single church in the Diocese had a visit from one of the Bishops at least once in three years. His visits of whatever kind were welcomed by the great majority of the clergy, and many of them knew him as the "homely" Bishop, for he was easy to entertain, bringing a special warmth as he talked with them and acted the fool with their children.

There were some who were slightly intimidated by his stern exterior, or even by his boisterousness, though he found this difficult to understand. "Afraid of me?" he would say in astonishment, if I suggested it to him, "afraid of me? I don't believe it, you're pulling my leg." He had a great sense of fun, willing to sing a comic song if an opportunity presented itself, using his gift of mimicry on many an occasion, and possessing a fund of stories with which he regaled his friends. There was often laughter in the air when he was present, and generally people felt better for having been in his company.

He did not wear his heart on his sleeve with regard to his own spirituality, but I knew he was up at six each morning, and before breakfast had said Morning Prayer and conducted his own devotions. By the time his secretaries arrived at nine, the mail had been opened, the answers were all on tape, and *The Times* crossword puzzle had been duly completed!

He was not beyond using a fairly mild expletive now and again, either for emphasis, for fun, or in an attempt to shock the over-pious. He could not entirely erase the years he had spent in the sergeants' mess and some of the vocabulary of those times remained. There was one celebrated occasion when we had dined together with the other Bishops at Lambeth Palace. The meal had been indifferent, though the ladies who had prepared it had been profusely thanked and praised, bringing forth a dutiful round of applause from us all. As we filed out of the impressive Guard Room, the scene of our festivities, an ebullient Victor made his way over to me, declaiming in his loud bass voice, "I could have done better on a bl**** primus stove." Alas, for once Victor's tongue was sharper than his eye. He had failed to spot the Archbishop standing by my side. He must have heard, yet he did not bat an eyelid. Like they say, you do not become Primate of all England unless you have all your chairs at home!

However, that incident lay in the future, as Victor took my right hand in his and led me to the Archbishop of York seated in front of the Altar in the Minster. Holding my other hand in the Presentation, was Patrick, Bishop of Manchester. "Most Reverend Father in God," they said together, "we present unto you this godly and well-learned man, to be Ordained and Consecrated Bishop."

Since Bishops are Consecrated only on Saints' Days, the date chosen was 1 May, the day the Church honours St Philip and St James, Apostles. It was good we had hit on a day when comparatively unimportant saints were commemorated, and I took comfort from the fact that the lesser as well as the greater are needed in the Apostolic ministry of Christ. If that brought reassurance, the same could not be said of the conditions inside the magnificent Cathedral. Practically everybody was literally shaking, not from the excitement and solemnity, but from the very low temperature. "Trying to heat this place is like trying to heat the County of Yorkshire," said the head verger, in a graphic if not original observation. "We have given up trying, so there is, I'm afraid, no heat being provided at all."

I had been warned about this by the Archbishop over the breakfast table. "If I were you," he had said, "I would go back to your room and put on your pyjama jacket under your shirt. No, I'm not joking, just being very practical." I obeyed, and was rewarded by at least avoiding a constant shiver that might have suggested terror. (I recalled that Charles I had worn two shirts for a similar reason on that January day when he had stood on the scaffold.) Another plus for the Archbishop, I decided, one of many he had chalked up during our stay with him. He and his wife had shown the four of us no little kindness in the previous twenty-four hours. One thing I had refused to do while under his roof, was to allow him to clean my shoes, though he had offered. How could I possibly allow the Primate of England to clean my shoes! I made do with a rub on the back of my trousers, each shoe in turn, as I walked down the corridor in Bishopthorpe to the dining-room for breakfast.

By some miracle I actually enjoyed the wonderful service. It was next-to-the-last Consecration conducted by Dr Donald Coggan in York, for soon he was to be translated to Canterbury where he clearly emerged as one of the outstanding Archbishops of modern times. From this time on, he nicknamed me his "Penultimate". I was grateful not to have been his last, for I would have hated to have been called "Ultimate", as in "last straw" — that would have been too close for comfort.

The lovely sense of relief when it was all over was golden and never to be forgotten. As usual on these occasions, the

Archbishop had entertained all the visiting Bishops and their wives to lunch in St. William College, by the side of the Minster. In an adjoining room were scores of special guests, both family and friends. But finally came the blessed time when they had all been greeted and fed, and when Joyce and I were able to get into my new official car, turn its nose south-westwards, and head for our new home in Chester.

It was one of those special times of intimacy, when there was no need to speak much, but we were both aware that a new life-style lay ahead. It was a lovely afternoon, cold and sharp, with bright spring sunshine flooding the M62. Traffic was light and the road straight.

I was conscious of the new pectoral cross hanging on my chest — the parish of St. Thomas, Halliwell had kindly provided it. Parishioners at Ashton-under-Lyne had bought cope and mitre. Joyce herself had insisted on giving me the episcopal ring: large and made of gold, it was set with the traditional amethyst stone. She had got a local jeweller in the parish to make it, giving him clear instructions. "Nothing fancy, keep it simple," she had told him.

"Did I tell you," she asked after we had travelled for an hour or so, "that the man who made your ring is Jewish?"

"No, I don't think you did. Rather nice that. Jesus was Jewish, so I can think of it as yet another link with Him."

"Why do Bishops always have an amethyst?"

"As far as I can gather, nobody really knows, but there are all kinds of guesses. For one thing it's a purple stone, so at least it tones in with the cassock and the stock. Purple was the colour for princes in the ancient world. That explanation doesn't appeal to me very much for obvious reasons."

I looked at the amethyst closely before going on. I took the right hand off the wheel and held it across for Joyce to inspect it too. "This is one of the precious stones mentioned in the Book of Revelation as being found in Heaven," I said. "A wide variety of precious stones are mentioned, like sapphires, emeralds, and so on, and then it says, 'and the twelfth stone is an amethyst'. Maybe the fact that it is linked to twelve, the number of the Apostles, gives it a special significance for Bishops. Bit tenuous, I know, but it's just possible."

"Anything else?" asked Joyce. "Anything more convincing?"

"Don't know about more convincing, but there is one explanation more attractive ... to me, at any rate ... and especially just now."

"Let's have it," said Joyce.

"Well, the word 'a-methyst' means literally 'without alcohol'. You remember how the first Apostles on the day of Pentecost were accused of being drunk, they were so full of enthusiasm and joy. Maybe the ring is meant to convey that message to its wearer. It's God's Spirit that will bring the power and the happiness. It says that I can be intoxicated, amethyst-style, without alcohol, relying on God's Spirit for stimulation and excitement. After all, St Paul tells us that one of the fruits of the Spirit is joy."

Joyce said, "I thought for a minute you were going to say that from now on you had to be teetotal. Let's hope your new job lives up to its promise."

"I'll say 'Amen' to that. If it's half as good as being a parish priest, I'll not complain."

"There's only one way to find out, isn't there? Like they say in the movies, 'Step on the gas'." She snuggled down more comfortably in the seat before she spoke again. "Thank goodness the razzmatazz is over. Won't it be lovely to get back to Chester ... I mean, get back home. Don't much fancy being a Bishop's wife, but that's not how I shall think of myself. In fact, I've never really thought of myself as a Vicar's wife. Quite honestly, I'm satisfied with just being your wife. OK?"

"Sure. Play your cards right and I might keep you on. Hope you've something tasty for tea."

"Some lovely boiled ham. How's that for the Ace of Hearts?"